The Renaissance
ARTISTS

With
HISTORY PROJECTS
for Kids

Diane C. Taylor

Nomad Press
A division of Nomad Communications
10 9 8 7 6 5 4 3 2 1

This book was manufactured by Friesens Book Division
Altona, MB, Canada
October 2018, Job #246315

ISBN Softcover: 978-1-61930-688-2
ISBN Hardcover: 978-1-61930-686-8

Educational Consultant, Marla Conn

Questions regarding the ordering of this book should be addressed to
Nomad Press
2456 Christian St.
White River Junction, VT 05001
www.nomadpress.net

Printed in Canada.

Titles in *The Renaissance for Kids* Series

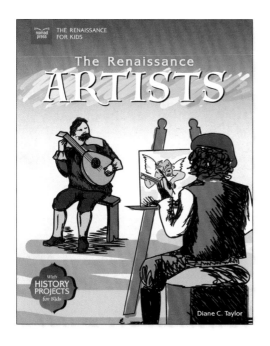

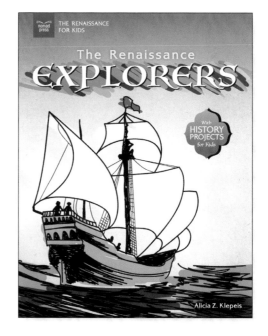

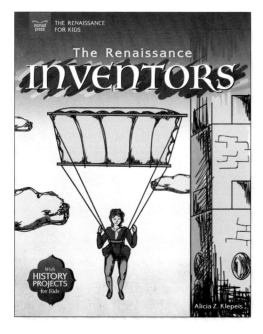

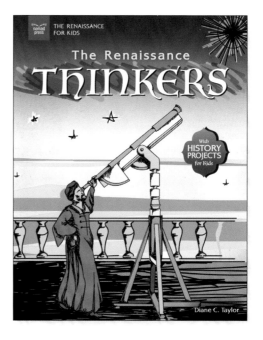

Check out more titles at www.nomadpress.net

TABLE OF
Contents

Introduction 1

The World of the Renaissance Artists

Chapter 1 11

Sandro Botticelli

Talented and Connected

Chapter 2 27

Leonardo da Vinci

A Revolutionary Artist, Inventor, and Scientist

Chapter 3   47
Michelangelo
Beauty and Artistic Achievement Beyond Imagination

****

Chapter 4   65
Raphael
Painting the Madonna

****

Chapter 5   83
Titian
The Early Appearance of Greatness

Glossary 98
Resources...................... 102
Index............................. 104

Mona Lisa
By Leonardo da Vinci,
painted between 1503 and 1507

THE WORLD OF THE
Renaissance Artists

Do you recognize these names? Botticelli. Leonardo. Michelangelo. Raphael. Titian. All five are famous Renaissance artists. Their sculptures and paintings are kept under guard in museums and cathedrals. Some pieces are even locked up behind bullet-proof glass! Have you seen the painting of the *Mona Lisa* by Leonardo da Vinci before? This is one of the most famous paintings of the Renaissance.

Cupid with Wheel of Fortune

By Titian, circa 1520

FAST FACTS

WHAT:
THE RENAISSANCE, A HISTORICAL ERA MARKED BY DRAMATIC CHANGE

WHEN: 1300s–1600s

WHERE:
ITALY AND NORTHERN EUROPE

While we might not be able to see and touch artwork made during the Renaissance every day, Renaissance art is all around us. It is woven into the fabric of our culture. It shows up in everything from coffee mugs to postage stamps.

Have you seen these cherubs before? They appear in a painting by Raphael from 1512, but they also turn up in many modern products, especially around the holidays. You might have seen them on greeting cards or dinner plates! Why do you think Renaissance art is still so popular with people today?

Defining the Renaissance

Renaissance is a French word that means rebirth. But what is the Renaissance? What was being reborn?

The Renaissance was a time when Europeans rediscovered the cultures of ancient Greece and Rome. They went in search of old texts, architecture, and art. What they found made a profound impact on how they thought.

For centuries, the Catholic Church had taught that the answers to all questions were found in the Bible. But as people studied what was written long before the rise of Christianity, they began to question that approach.

The Parthenon is a temple dedicated to the goddess Athena. It's a great example of the culture and creativity of the ancient Greeks.

Renaissance Art
1300s–1600s

1434
Jan van Eyck paints the *Arnolfini Portrait.*

1482
Sandro Botticelli paints *Primavera.*

1495
Leonardo da Vinci paints *The Last Supper.*

Hieronymus Bosch paints *The Garden of Earthly Delights.*

1498
Albrecht Dürer creates the woodblock print *The Four Horsemen of the Apocalypse.*

1504 Michelangelo sculpts the *David* statue.

1508 Michelangelo paints the ceiling of the Sistine Chapel.

1511 Raphael paints *The School of Athens* in the Vatican apartments.

1515 Titian paints the *Assumption of the Virgin* in Venice.

1534 Titian paints the *Venus of Urbino*.

1566 Pieter Bruegel the Elder paints *The Peasant Wedding*.

APPRENTICESHIPS

Renaissance artists learned their craft by working and living with a master artist. Called apprenticeships, these work terms lasted from three to seven years. Apprentices were often called upon to work in different ways, such as painting, sculpting, and even creating glassware! Some children were placed with an apprentice before they turned 10 years old. An apprenticeship usually took the place of any other formal education.

During the Renaissance, people in Europe saw that ancient civilizations had accomplished amazing things in mathematics, literature, and science. The "rebirth" took place when Europeans applied that lost knowledge to their own times.

The Renaissance began in Italy in the city-state of Florence around the year 1350. It spread throughout Europe as people traveled and shared ideas about science, exploration, philosophy, and art.

By the late 1600s, though, an economic downturn meant that people had less money to spend on supporting cultural hobbies such as art. Wars, disease, and a wave of new ideas about religion were all reasons the Renaissance gradually ended.

> "Something happened in the Renaissance, something that surged up against the constraints that centuries had constructed around curiosity, desire, individuality, (and) sustained attention to the material world."
>
> STEPHEN GREENBLATT, *THE SWERVE: HOW THE WORLD BECAME MODERN*

Humanism

The Renaissance was a time of discovery, of new ideas and new ways of thinking. The new approach to learning was called humanism. The people who pursued it were called humanists.

Humanists still believed in God, but they also believed that truth existed outside the Bible. They sought knowledge among the writings of the ancient Greeks and Romans, for example, and showed respect to God by uncovering the mysteries of the world.

For Renaissance artists, this meant paying close attention to the world around them. They studied everything in great detail, including plants, animals, machines, human beings—even fruit. In much of their art, these artists tried to reveal things as they truly existed. As a result, they started doing things in art that had not been done for thousands of years.

Medieval Art

What was European art like before the Renaissance?

The period of time before the Renaissance was called the Middle Ages, or the medieval era. The Middle Ages began at the end of the Roman Empire, lasting from about the year 470 to the 1300s.

Maiolica Basket of Fruit

By Fede Galizia, 1610s

Medieval art was found mostly in churches. Its main purpose was to illustrate Christian stories. Artists painted and sculpted Christian figures, such as Jesus and the Virgin Mary.

Medieval art can be elaborate and beautiful. It is frequently embellished with gold leaf. But it is also very predictable and often looks very similar to other pieces of art. The Virgin Mary always has the same face. Saint Peter always has a key. Saint Catherine always has a wheel, and so on.

Why was this done? These images, known as icons, took the guesswork out of understanding art. Medieval art was made in a way that nearly everyone understood, so that people could direct their attention to their prayers.

WONDER WHY?

Every culture has its own artistic traditions. Have you seen art from Africa, Asia, or Central and South America? How does art reflect culture?

Today, art often encourages viewers to ask questions and think harder about themselves and their surroundings. Why do you think the purpose of art has changed so much since medieval times?

The Human Body in Renaissance Art

Many artists continued to create religious images that closely resembled artwork from the Middle Ages. Others, however, turned away from creating religious icons. Remember, during the Renaissance, people rediscovered the work of the ancient Greeks and Romans.

The ancient Greeks and Romans had been realists. Renaissance artists wanted to explore ways of painting and sculpting the world in a realistic way, especially when it came to the human body.

This means that there's a lot of nudity in Renaissance art. This has always made some people uncomfortable.

But the artists saw beauty in the naked human body. To them, it was another way to show their faith in God, who, according to the Bible, created humans. Renaissance artists tried to express divine perfection in the human form.

COMPARE AND CONTRAST

Here are two religious paintings of the Virgin Mary and Child.

One is by the medieval painter Duccio (unknown–1319). The other is by the Renaissance painter Raphael (1483–1520).

Can you tell which is which?

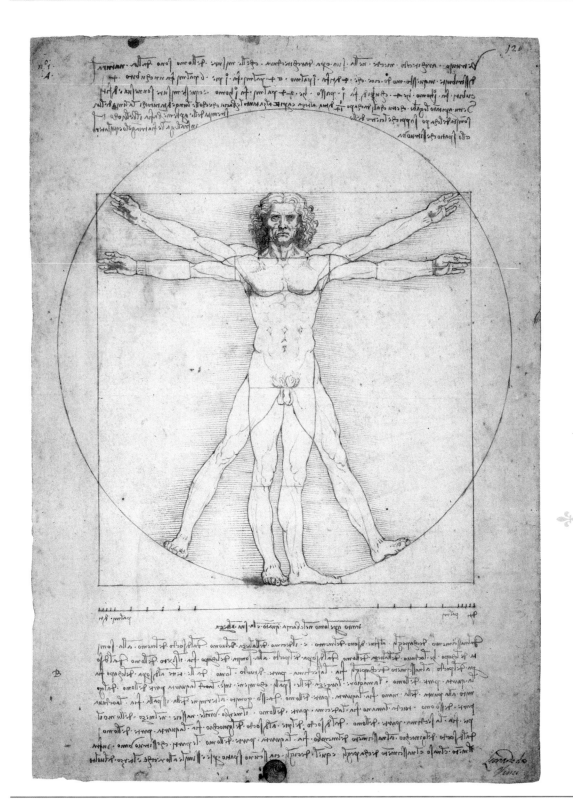

The Vitruvian Man

A study of the proportions of the human body by Leonardo da Vinci. It was drawn around 1490.

Changing the Subject

Renaissance artists experimented with new subjects. Humanist patrons wanted art that explored themes in mythology, ancient history, and everyday life. Portraits were another new development.

Before the Renaissance, painted portraits were few and far between. Royalty, religious leaders, and wealthy individuals had their portraits made. Ordinary people did not. Why do you think this was the case?

During the Renaissance, however, many more people had portraits done. A booming economy created new forms of wealth. For those who could afford it, having a portrait painted became a symbol of wealth.

CONNECT

Learn about ancient Greece and the Parthenon in this video. What structures that are built today might be standing in another 3,000 years?

🔍 **Ancient Greece Videos**

Portrait of a Gentleman

By Altobello Melone, between 1500 and 1524

WONDER WHY?

Do you have portraits of yourself or family members? Do you take selfies? Do you have posters of famous people? How is this similar to having your portrait painted during the Renaissance?

There's another reason portraits became popular during the Renaissance. Artists began to focus on human beings as unique individuals. They created natural, emotional portraits that made viewers feel as though they were seeing people in real life.

Artist as Celebrity

Medieval artists had tried to keep their personalities out of their art. They rarely signed their names, for example. They felt that the goal of art was to glorify God. A person's name in the artwork was a needless distraction.

In contrast, Renaissance artists highlighted their own individuality through their art. They signed their work and even included self-portraits! They modeled characters from the Bible, mythology, and history on their own faces, as well as those of their patrons.

"The greatest works of (the Renaissance) exude confidence, a heroic vision of man . . . as the summit of God's creation."

MILES J. UNGER, *MICHELANGELO: A LIFE IN SIX MASTERPIECES*

EARNING A LIVING

Renaissance artists worked on commission. Customers, called patrons, hired artists to paint pictures or make sculptures of certain things or people. They drew up detailed legal contracts for what they wanted. If artists failed to make the art the patron had hired them for, the artists could be sued! How is this different from being the kind of artist who makes whatever art they want to make?

Meet the Stars

In *The Renaissance Artists*, you will dive deep into the biographies of five famous artists and meet other artists from the period, including those from Italy and northern Europe. You'll also discover some women who managed to make art despite the attitude of the time that careers were for men.

As a group and as individuals, these men and women changed the way people thought about art. Maybe they'll change how you think about it!

Adoration of the Magi
Self-portrait by Botticelli,
circa 1475

CHAPTER 1

SANDRO Botticelli

Portrait of a Young Woman

By Sandro Botticelli,
circa 1480–1485

Take one look at a painting by Sandro Botticelli, and you know you have left the artistic traditions of medieval Europe. Botticelli painted religious images, but they were not icons. What's more, he accepted major commissions for paintings based on classical mythology.

FAST FACTS

BIRTH DATE: 1445

PLACE OF BIRTH: ITALY

AGE AT DEATH: 65

**PLACE OF BURIAL:
OGNISSANTI CHAPEL,
FLORENCE, ITALY**

FAMOUS ARTWORKS:
- *ADORATION OF THE MAGI*
- *PRIMAVERA*
- *THE BIRTH OF VENUS*

With his naturalistic Christian paintings, Botticelli built on the work of earlier Renaissance artists. However, his mythological paintings introduced something almost entirely new.

Early Years

Botticelli was born into a working-class family in Florence. His father's name was Mariano di Vanni d'Amedeo Filipepi. But we know the painter as Sandro Botticelli. Why are their names so different?

No one knows for sure. Some say that when Sandro was 14 years old, he studied with a goldsmith named Botticelli, and that he later adopted the master's last name. Others say that it started as a nickname, and that it stuck with Sandro because he resembled what *botticello* means in Italian—"little barrel."

Still others suggest the nickname was somehow derived from Botticelli's older brother. Whatever the case may be, Botticelli worked with the goldsmith for just a short time. In 1462, Botticelli went to work with artist Fra Filippo Lippi (c. 1406–1469) for seven or eight years. Fra Filippo Lippi was Botticelli's main teacher.

> ". . . (Botticelli) refused to settle down or be satisfied with reading, writing, and arithmetic; and, finally, exasperated by his son's restless mind, his father apprenticed him to a goldsmith . . . ."
>
> GIORGIO VASARI (1511–1574), *LIVES OF THE ARTISTS*

Botticelli
1445–1510

1445	1459	1461	1470	1475
Sandro Botticelli is born in Florence.	Botticelli apprentices to a goldsmith.	Botticelli apprentices to the artist Fra Filippo Lippi.	He moves into the house that will be his home and studio for the rest of his life.	He paints *Adoration of the Magi* in the church of Santa Maria Novella.

Botticelli's Teacher

Orphaned as a young child, Filippo Lippi was raised by nuns in a convent. When he was a teenager, he became a friar of the Carmelite order of Catholic monks. That's when he added the word *Fra* to his name, which means "brother" in Italian.

Fra Filippo Lippi's most famous works are a series of murals in the Prato Cathedral, near Florence. He painted scenes from the lives of two Biblical figures—Saint John the Baptist and Saint Stephen.

A close-up of the woman dancing in Fra Filippo Lippi's *Feast of Herod*, located in the Prato Cathedral

Art historians believe this image influenced Botticelli's *Primavera* and *The Birth of Venus*, circa 1452–1464

1481
Botticelli travels to Rome to paint wall frescoes in the Sistine Chapel.

1482
He completes *Primavera* for the Medici family.

1486
Botticelli completes *The Birth of Venus* for an unknown patron.

1490s
The activist monk Girolamo Savonarola speaks out against the artwork of the times.

1500
Botticelli paints *The Mystical Nativity*, most likely for personal use rather than as a commission.

1510
Botticelli dies of old age in Florence.

Art Close to Home

Botticelli lived nearly his entire life within a few miles of where he was born. By the time he was 25, Botticelli was living in a house that his father had purchased. That property became Botticelli's combined home and studio until the day he died.

Fortunately for Botticelli, Florence was a great place to be an artist. The work of cloth merchants and bankers had turned Florence into one of the wealthiest city-states in all of Italy. With money to spare, Florentine families spent generously on art to adorn churches and government buildings and to beautify their private palaces.

One of the richest and most powerful of those families was the Medici. And it was another man's desire to gain favor with the Medici that resulted in Botticelli receiving one of his most important early commissions in 1475—the *Adoration of the Magi*.

CONNECT

Botticelli worked exclusively with tempera. This is a paint made from mixing together egg yolks, water, and finely ground pigments for color. Watch an artist make and paint with egg tempera. How might this be different from painting with watercolors?

 egg tempera demonstration

Adoration of the Magi

This painting originally adorned a chapel in Florence. The *Adoration of the Magi* now hangs in the Uffizi Gallery, also in Florence. The painting was commissioned by Gaspare di Zanobi del Lama, a banker and business associate of another influential Florentine family—the Medici.

The scene of the adoration of the magi is a common theme in Christian art. It is based on a story from the New Testament of the Bible. Jesus has been born. Three kings, the magi, come to worship the child and offer him gifts. Also in the painting are the Virgin Mary, Joseph, and others who have come to honor the Christ child.

WONDER WHY?

Is it important for art to be realistic? Are there thoughts, feelings, or scenes that can be portrayed more accurately if they are less realistic?

"The [*Adoration of the Magi*] is remarkable for the emotion shown by the elderly man as he kisses the foot of Our Lord with wonderful tenderness and conveys his sense of relief at having come to the end of his long journey."

GIORGIO VASARI, *LIVES OF THE ARTISTS*

Adoration of the Magi, circa 1476

Tempera on a wood panel, 44 inches by 53 inches. Can you spot Botticelli's self-portrait?

The Botticelli Brothers

So little is known about Botticelli's personal life, he often seems a man alone. He never married or had children, nor was he known for any great romances.

RENAISSANCE WOMEN

Levina Teerlinc (1510–1576) was born in Belgium and was trained as a manuscript painter by her father, the artist Simon Bening (1483–1561). As an adult, she married and moved to England with her husband. There, she became a painter in the English royal court. Her specialty was miniature portraits, small enough to hold in the palm of your hand. The English court paid Teerlinc a large salary, and she trained the artist Nicholas Hilliard (1547–1619) in her methods. Hilliard's miniatures of English royalty made him one of the most important artists of his time, and many of his paintings survive today. Sadly, most of Teerlinc's paintings were either destroyed in a palace fire in 1691 or otherwise lost.

Miniature portrait of Elizabeth I of England

By Levina Teerlinc, circa 1565

However, he did have three older brothers—Antonio, Giovanni, and Simone—and it may have been Antonio who cleared a path for Sandro to become an artist. In 1460, Antonio found work beating out gold leaf, the ultra-thin sheets of real gold that adorned much religious art. Such work put Antonio in regular contact with Florentine artists. This made it more likely that his younger brother Sandro would be able to secure an apprenticeship.

Art and Inspiration

While painting frescoes for the Sistine Chapel in Rome, Botticelli immersed himself in Christian themes. But when he returned to Florence in May 1482, his art took a dramatic turn toward classical mythology.

Botticelli accepted a new commission from the Medici family. His subject was the arrival of spring, which he depicted in a most unchristian-like fashion. Gone are the Virgin Mary and the baby Jesus. In their place are Venus and Cupid.

**Primavera,
1482**

Tempera on a
wood panel,
124 inches by
80 inches

Primavera was unlike anything Botticelli had ever painted before. But we can't give Botticelli all the credit for creating something so strikingly original. Botticelli's patrons, the Medici family, deserve some credit, too. After all, they commissioned the work. It was the Medici's interest in the ancient myths of Greece and Rome that inspired Botticelli to explore new themes in art.

Primavera

Originally adorning a private home, *Primavera* is now displayed in the Uffizi Gallery in Florence. The Medici family commissioned *Primavera* as a wedding gift for a member of the family.

Primavera, which means "spring" in Italian, is one of several Botticelli paintings based on classical mythology. It's a complex, mysterious painting.

In *Primavera*, Venus, the goddess of love and beauty, stands at the center of an orange grove. Her son, Cupid, is the blindfolded cherub in the tree. To the far left is Mercury, the god of the month of May. The three women dancing are the Graces. They represent chastity, beauty, and love.

To the far right is Zephyr, the god of the west wind. The woman in the flowered dress is Flora, the goddess of spring.

The Birth of Venus

The Birth of Venus, 1486

Painted with tempera on a canvas that measures 109 inches by 69 inches

No one knows who commissioned another of Botticelli's famous paintings, *The Birth of Venus*. But it came into the possession of the Medici family sometime before 1550, and now hangs in the Uffizi Gallery.

In this painting, Venus stands on a giant shell at the edge of the ocean. To her right, Flora prepares to cover her with a robe. On her left, the god of the west wind, Zephyr, and his mate, Chloris, blow a gentle breeze. The wind scatters flowers in Venus' direction and also blows through her hair.

> "Botticelli's willful departures from reality . . . creat(e) a parallel world which is purer and more beautiful than the one we live in."
>
> TOM NICHOLS, *RENAISSANCE ART: A BEGINNER'S GUIDE*

WHO ASKED FOR A NAKED WOMAN?

Four years after *Primavera*, Botticelli branched out in yet another direction. In *The Birth of Venus*, he painted the first known female nude since antiquity. Was it his idea to portray Venus as a naked woman or did that idea come from a patron? We can't really say, because no one knows for sure who commissioned this painting! It did eventually wind up in the Medici family collection of art, so it might have been the Medici who once again prompted Botticelli to create something daringly original.

Greek Influences in Renaissance Art

In *The Birth of Venus*, Botticelli turned to ancient Greece for inspiration. One of the most famous ancient Greek sculptures is the *Aphrodite of Knidos* by Praxiteles (395–330 BCE). It is a full-body sculpture of the Greek goddess of love. This pose has been copied many times. It became known as a *Venus pudica*, or "modest Venus."

Botticelli clearly modeled his Venus on Praxiteles's work. Unlike Praxiteles, however, Botticelli did not give his Venus a realistic human body. Do you see how long her left arm is and how it attaches to her shoulder? That's a very oddly shaped human arm!

CONNECT

Sister Wendy is a nun and accomplished art critic. Listen to her views on *The Birth of Venus*

🔍 **Sister Wendy Birth of Venus**

Copy of *Aphrodite*
Ippolito Buzzi
(1562–1634)

WONDER WHY?

How does the subject influence what an artist creates? Does the subject determine what colors, textures, and materials the artist will use?

JAN VAN EYCK

While much of the Renaissance was centered around Italy, great art was being produced in other areas of the world as well. In the northern country of Belgium, Jan van Eyck (circa 1390–1441) was a master painter who also served as a diplomat. He is considered to be one of the prime representatives of the Northern Renaissance. One of his most famous paintings is the *Arnolfini Portrait*. In this double portrait of a married couple, Jan van Eyck did something new in Western art. He made a totally nonreligious painting of two ordinary people in an ordinary room. Van Eyck was also one of the first Europeans to use oil paint rather than tempera in his art.

Possible Regrets

Not everyone in Florence approved of artistic innovation. One man especially, a Dominican monk named Girolamo Savonarola (1452–1498), feared that people were going morally astray. To him, the fact that artists were painting Venus rather than the Virgin Mary was a sign that people were losing their religion.

> **"Spring comes and Venus, preceded by Venus's winged harbinger, and mother Flora, following hard on the heels of Zephyr, prepares the way for them, strewing all their path with a profusion of exquisite hues and scents."**
>
> *ON THE NATURE OF THINGS*, BY LUCRETIUS, ANCIENT GREEK POET

From 1490 to 1498, Savonarola delivered passionate speeches that rallied people to repent of their sins. One famous event he caused was the Bonfire of the Vanities in 1497. On that night, large crowds gathered around an enormous bonfire and threw in their vain, worldly possessions—jewelry, fancy clothes, books, and art.

CONNECT

Listen to experts discuss the technique and significance of the *Arnolfini Portrait*.

 smart history Arnolfini

For centuries, it was said that Botticelli tossed his own paintings into Savonarola's fire. We have no proof that he did. But Botticelli was a religious man, and his brother Simone definitely was a follower of Savonarola. Even if he didn't destroy any paintings, Botticelli may have felt some unease over the less religious works of art that he created.

Statue of Savonarola in Ferrara, Italy

IN AFRICA

While Botticelli explored new themes in classical mythology, the Dogon people of Mali, in West Africa, continued a long artistic tradition of sculpting in wood. As with Renaissance art of the same time period, Dogon art was primarily concerned with religious themes. Unlike their counterparts in Europe, however, the Dogon did not display their religious art in public. The symbolism of the art was considered to be powerful and mysterious. The Dogon felt it was best to keep such items hidden in their homes or in the safekeeping of their top religious leader, the hogon. The Dogon people are still famous for their art today. The areas where they live are some of Mali's most popular tourist attractions.

Dogon sculpture of a kneeling woman

WONDER WHY?

Is there an artist from the past whose work you enjoy? Is there an artist whose work you wish you could imitate?

Botticelli's Legacy

We may never know how Botticelli himself felt about his own work. As he aged, however, it seems that patrons found his work increasingly less appealing. In the final years of his life, he supposedly could no longer support himself as an artist. He stopped receiving commissions from the Medici family. He may even have lived on the charity of others.

For a long time after Botticelli died, his work continued to be underappreciated. The incredible realism in works by artists such as Leonardo da Vinci and Michelangelo overshadowed Botticelli's more playful and poetic paintings.

> "I wear myself out trying to render the orange trees so that they're not stiff but like those I saw by Botticelli in Florence. It's a dream that won't come true."
>
> **BERTHE MORISOT (1841-1895), FRENCH PAINTER**

For hundreds of years, there was little public interest in Botticelli's art. Private collectors who wanted to sell their Botticelli pieces had a hard time finding people to buy them.

In the early 1900s, that changed. From 1900 to 1920, for example, more books were written about Botticelli than any other painter. Today, a private collector with an original Botticelli painting would find many buyers.

The Temptations of Christ, **1481**

BOTTICELLI IN ROME

In 1481, Pope Sixtus IV (1414–1484) commissioned several Florentine artists to decorate the walls of the Sistine Chapel in Rome. Botticelli completed three paintings—*Events of the Life of Moses, The Temptations of Christ,* and *The Punishment of Korah.* Historians believe this is the only time Botticelli spent outside his hometown of Florence.

Analyze a Work of Art

Botticelli painted a few versions of the *Adoration of the Magi*. Take a look at this version and compare it to the version on page 15, which was painted earlier.

➤ **As you study the two paintings, ask yourself these questions.**

- What is similar about these two paintings? Can you tell they were both painted by Botticelli? If so, how?

- What is different about these two paintings? Why do you think the painter created these differences?

- Why might an artist paint the same scene more than once? Can you think of other examples in art?

Botticelli's 1478–1482 version of the *Adoration of the Magi*, which now hangs in the National Gallery of Art, Washington, DC

Try This!

➤ **Create your own series of art that is focused on the same subject.** You might choose to paint, draw, take pictures, write a poem, or build a structure. Do at least five versions of the same subject.

- What do you notice about your subject the fifth time you use it that you didn't notice the first time?

- How is your last version different from your first?

- What do you think would happen if you tackled this topic even more times? What might change about your artwork?

Compare and Contrast

Take a look at two paintings of the Nativity. Both depict Jesus soon after he was born, but one is by the medieval artist Lorenzo Monaco (1370–1425), the other is by Botticelli.

Lorenzo Monaco, *The Nativity*

Botticelli, *The Mystical Nativity*

> ➤ **Consider the paintings and then think about these questions.**

- Can you tell which is which? How?
- Is one painting more naturalistic than the other?
- Which composition is more complex?
- Does one painting focus your attention on religious devotion more than the other?
- Which painting requires more time and attention to figure out what's going on?
- What do you think is the biggest difference between the medieval and the Renaissance Nativity?

WORDS OF WONDER

What vocabulary words did you discover? Can you figure out the meanings of these words by using the context and roots? Look in the glossary for help!

convent · mural · fresco innovation · repent · charity

Project

Responding to *The Birth of Venus*

Countless visual artists have responded to Botticelli's *The Birth of Venus* by remaking the painting into works of art that reflects their own ideas. Photographer Angela Strassheim (1969–), for example, staged Venus rising from a blue plastic kiddie pool. Japanese artist Tomoko Nagao (1976–) pictured Venus standing in the center of a gaming console.

Botticelli, *The Birth of Venus*

➤ **What do you think inspires artists to remake this particular work of art?** Why are so many people drawn to it? What does it represent? Why does it remain important?

➤ **When you look at *The Birth of Venus*, what do you see?** How would you respond to this painting if you were to make it into something new?

➤ **Create you own response to this painting.** If you are a visual artist, you might make a painting, a sculpture, or a panorama. If you're not, then perhaps you might write a short story, a poem, or a song that is inspired by *The Birth of Venus*. You might also try being an art critic and write a review of Botticelli's *The Birth of Venus* or of another artist's remake.

➤ **Whatever form your response takes, ask yourself this when you're done.** How did your understanding of Botticelli's *The Birth of Venus* change as you responded to it with your own creative efforts?

CONNECT

Check out these modern variations on Botticelli's *The Birth of Venus*.

🔍 **Oddee Birth of Venus**

Portrait of Leonardo da Vinci
Believed to be a self-portrait,
circa 1505

CHAPTER 2

LEONARDO
da Vinci

Leonardo da Vinci
Self-portrait

Leonardo da Vinci is regarded as one of the most accomplished artists who ever lived. But do you know how many paintings he actually finished? Most Renaissance artists produced dozens, even hundreds, of paintings.

Leonardo completed 15.

FAST FACTS

BIRTH DATE: 1452

PLACE OF BIRTH:
VINCI, ITALY

AGE AT DEATH: 67

PLACE OF BURIAL:
CHAPEL OF SAINT-HUBERT,
AMBOISE, FRANCE

FAMOUS ARTWORKS:
- *THE ADORATION OF*
  THE MAGI
- THE *VIRGIN OF THE ROCKS*
- *THE LAST SUPPER*
- *MONA LISA*

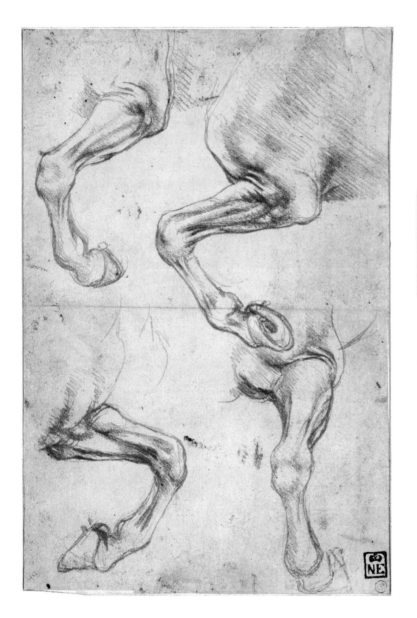

However, Leonardo made thousands of drawings. He was always drawing something—horses, birds, human faces, human body parts, weapons, machines, cats, flowing water, and buildings.

> **"Drawing seems to have been almost second nature to him."**
>
> **SERGE BRAMLY, *LEONARDO: THE ARTIST AND THE MAN***

He kept his drawings in notebooks, and they don't count as his finished works. Yet today, even Leonardo's simple sketches are admired for their artistry and attention to detail. His drawings of the human heart are so precise, doctors have used them to assist in heart surgeries.

Leonardo, equestrian sketches

Leonardo
1452–1519

1452
Leonardo da Vinci is born in Vinci, Italy.

1466
He studies with Verrocchio in Florence.

1480
Leonardo begins, but does not finish, *Saint Jerome in the Wilderness*.

1481
He starts another painting, *Adoration of the Magi*, without finishing it.

1482
Leonardo moves to Milan.

Early Years

Leonardo was born to an unwed mother in the rural village of Vinci. His mother's name was Caterina.

He was brought up by his biological father, the lawyer Piero Fruosino di Antonio da Vinci (1427–1504), and his stepmother, Albiera Amadori (dates unknown).

Being born to unmarried parents greatly influenced Leonardo's life. Under different circumstances, he might have followed in the profession of his father. But at that time, the guild for lawyers barred illegitimate children from joining the organization.

Leonardo had to find another way to earn a living. Fortunately, he showed artistic ability at a young age. When he was 14, his father apprenticed him to Verrocchio (c. 1435–1488), one of the leading Florentine artists of his day.

WONDER WHY?

What obstacles to beginning a career do some people face today? Does it matter who your parents are? Are there organizations you have to join to be successful?

Leonardo's Teacher

Verrocchio's given name was Andrea di Michele di Francesco de' Cioni. But everybody called him Verrocchio. In Italian, *vero occhio* means "true eye." That nickname was a compliment to Verrocchio's talent.

> **"The human foot is a masterpiece of engineering and a work of art."**
>
> **LEONARDO DA VINCI**

1485	1495	1505	1510	1513	1516	1519
He paints *The Virgin of the Rocks*.	He paints *The Last Supper*.	Leonardo begins, but does not finish, *The Battle of Anghiari* fresco in Florence.	He spends his time working on *Mona Lisa*.	*St. John the Baptist* is his final painting.	Leonardo moves to France.	Leonardo dies in France.

Do you think of an artist as someone working alone in a studio? That may be the way art is produced today. But during the Renaissance, a successful artist's studio was a busy and crowded place. It was called a bottega.

Verrocchio ran an exceptionally busy bottega. The leading families of Florence commissioned him to produce everything from paintings to buildings. To get all that work done, he took in many students and hired lots of assistants.

Verrocchio himself was most accomplished as a sculptor. His masterpiece is the equestrian statue of Bartolomeo Colleoni (1395–1475), which stands in Venice.

Leonardo qualified as a master artist and joined a guild by the time he turned 20. His father set him up with a bottega of his own in Florence. Yet he continued to work alongside Verrocchio for five or six more years.

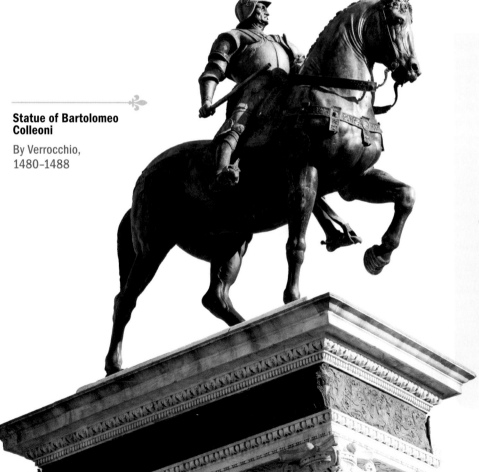

Statue of Bartolomeo Colleoni

By Verrocchio, 1480–1488

"It was because of his profound knowledge of painting that Leonardo started so many things without finishing them; he was convinced that his hands . . . could never perfectly express the subtle and wonderful ideas of his imagination."

GIORGIO VASARI, *LIVES OF THE ARTISTS*

Unfinished Business

In 1481, Leonardo accepted a commission to produce the *Adoration of the Magi* for a group of monks in Florence. He set to work on the painting. But within a year, he moved to Milan and abandoned the work.

Throughout his career, Leonardo failed to finish many commissions. No one can say for sure why. But in the case of the *Adoration of the Magi*, an unfortunate run-in with the law may explain why he moved from Florence and left that painting unfinished.

In 1476, Florentine authorities accused Leonardo of homosexuality. Under both religious and secular laws, homosexuality was illegal. If found guilty, Leonardo could have been imprisoned or even executed.

The charges against Leonardo were eventually dropped. But it was an unsettling incident all the same. He sought a new start for himself in Milan.

THE TROUBLE WITH ORIGINALITY

The sheer originality of Leonardo's art may provide yet another clue as to why he abandoned his work on the *Adoration of the Magi*. Leonardo's *Adoration of the Magi* was very untraditional, almost strange. It included battle scenes with men on rearing horses. It showed people in great emotional distress. The initial drawings were so odd, it's possible that Leonardo never completed the painting because the monks wanted nothing to do with it!

Leonardo's preliminary drawing of the *Adoration of the Magi* is shown here. Compare it to Botticelli's *Adoration of the Magi* on page 15. How are the two pieces different?

WONDER WHY?

Have you ever encountered artwork that made you uncomfortable?

LEONARDO'S LOST HORSE

The largest—and in some ways the most heartbreaking—commission that Leonardo never completed was a bronze sculpture of a horse and rider that became known as the *Gran Cavallo*, or *Great Horse*. The Duke of Milan, Ludovico Sforza (1452–1508), commissioned the piece as a monument to his deceased father. And had Leonardo been able to complete the work, it would have been the largest equestrian statue of the Renaissance period.

Unfortunately, Leonardo never got beyond the making of an enormous clay model. Duke Sforza had set aside 70 tons of bronze for the statue. But when Milan was threatened with an invasion from France in 1494, Sforza ordered the bronze to be used to make cannons to defend the city. In later years, Michelangelo would ridicule Leonardo for having failed to complete the *Gran Cavallo*.

"Art is never finished, only abandoned."

LEONARD DA VINCI

Portrait of Ludovico Sforza
By Giovanni Ambrogio de Predis, dates unknown

Leonardo in Milan

When Leonardo first arrived in Milan, he was more interested in being a military engineer than an artist. In a letter to the Duke of Milan, Ludovico Sforza, Leonardo listed 10 ways that he could help the duke protect his territory. Leonardo boasted that he could "invent an infinite variety of machines for both attack and defense."

Only at the end of the letter does Leonardo mention his artistic abilities. In times of peace, he said he could "carry out sculpture in marble, bronze, and clay; and in painting can do any kind of work as well as any man . . . ."

He might have undersold himself as a painter. In 1483, he began work on one of his most remarkable paintings, *The Virgin of the Rocks.*

The Virgin of the Rocks

The Virgin of the Rocks was commissioned by a charitable religious organization called the Confraternity of the Immaculate Conception. The painting originally adorned a chapel inside the San Francesco Grande church in Milan. Today, it is in the Louvre in Paris, France.

The Virgin of the Rocks is Leonardo's version of a medieval legend about John the Baptist and Jesus. According to the story, the two meet as infants soon after the birth of Jesus. An angel brings John to meet Jesus while Jesus and his family are traveling from Bethlehem to Egypt.

The Virgin Mary is in the center, with John the Baptist at her right. His hands are folded in prayer and pointed at Jesus. Jesus is making the sign of a blessing to John. The figure behind Jesus is the angel who brought John to Jesus.

The Virgin of the Rocks, 1485
Oil on a wood panel, 48 inches by 78 inches

While the theme for Leonardo's *The Virgin of the Rocks* wasn't new, his materials and techniques were. Not only was Leonardo one of the first Italian artists to adopt oil as his preferred medium, in *The Virgin of the Rocks* he also pioneered a style called sfumato.

In Italian, *fumo* means "smoke," and in sfumato painting, lines become difficult to see, as if they are blurred in a cloud of smoke. Figures seem to emerge and become visible from a darkness that surrounds them.

The Duke of Milan

Leonardo kept busy working for the duke in the 15 years that he lived in Milan, but not always with painting. Rulers such as Sforza liked to show off their wealth by entertaining people with lavish parades, festivals, and theatrical productions. Such grand spectacles called for elaborate costumes and clever stage sets that could have actors seeming to fly through the air or suddenly disappear.

"In [the apostles'] faces, one can read the emotions of love, dismay, and anger, or rather sorrow, at their failure to grasp the meaning of Christ."

GIORGIO VASARI, *LIVES OF THE ARTISTS*

Those were the types of projects on which the duke most often called upon Leonardo to work. In 1494, however, he asked Leonardo to paint a mural. *The Last Supper* now adorns a wall in the dining hall of the convent of Santa Maria delle Grazie in Milan.

The Last Supper captures the moment when Jesus tells his 12 apostles that one of them will betray him. The scene takes place after dinner on the night before Jesus is crucified. Jesus is standing at the center of the table. All 12 apostles react to the disturbing news.

The Last Supper, 1495
A combination of oil and tempera on a plaster wall, 350 inches by 180 inches.

> "[*The Last Supper*] was so finely composed and executed that the King of France . . . wanted to remove it to his kingdom. . . . But as the painting was done on a wall his majesty failed to have his way. . . ."
>
> **GIORGIO VASARI, *LIVES OF THE ARTISTS***

Leonardo's Experiment

Leonardo was always experimenting with new techniques. Sometimes they worked. Sometimes they didn't. When he painted *The Last Supper*, he used a combination of oil and tempera that he had never used before on a dry plaster wall. Even before the mural was finished, the paint was fading, cracking, and peeling.

Santa Maria delle Grazie in Milan, where *The Last Supper* is installed.

CONNECT

Find out who's who in *The Last Supper* in this video.

🔍 **Smarthistory Last Supper**

The Last Supper, nearly destroyed during World War II bombings, remains on the wall of Santa Maria delle Grazie. While the painting has undergone numerous restorations, it will never regain its original colors.

Wandering Years

From 1499 to 1516, Leonardo lived in several Italian cities. In Venice and Cesena, he found work as a military architect and engineer. He designed defenses and created some of the first detailed maps of Italy.

He returned to Florence for a while, both to accept important art commissions (which he failed to complete) and to sort out the family estate after the death of his father. He went to Milan again, and lived for a time in Rome, where he became friends with Pope Leo X (1475–1521) and the new ruler of France, King Francis I (1494–1547).

> **"I have offended God and mankind because my work did not reach the quality it should have."**
>
> **LEONARDO DA VINCI**

LITTLE DEMON

Like several other Italian Renaissance artists, Leonardo never married and never had any children. But in 1490, he did take a 10-year-old boy into his house as a servant and a pupil. The child's name was Gian Giacomo Caprotti de Oreno (1480–1524), and he became a constant presence in Leonardo's life.

Giacomo was quite a mischievous character! Leonardo once used the words "thief," "liar," "obstinate," and "greedy" to describe him. His nickname, Salai, means "demon" in Tuscan Italian. But Salai was also a beautiful boy who became a handsome man, and Leonardo frequently used him as a model.

Whatever trouble Salai may have caused, Leonardo clearly loved him. He dressed the young Salai in the finest clothes, built a house for the adult Salai to live in, and left him a vineyard in his will.

At some point in his travels, most likely sometime after 1503, Leonardo began work on a portrait of a woman. Today, the *Mona Lisa* is on display behind bulletproof glass at the Louvre in Paris. It's not known for certain who—if anyone—commissioned this painting.

In the painting, a woman is seated in a chair, with her hands folded across her lap. She looks directly at the viewer. A faint smile is on her lips. She is posed in front of a rugged, dark, and wild landscape not known to be modeled after a real place.

Mona Lisa, circa 1503–1506
Oil on a poplar panel,
21 inches by 28 inches

The question of who asked Leonardo to paint the *Mona Lisa* is one of the biggest mysteries in art history. No one knows for certain. The best guess is that it is a portrait of Lisa del Giocondo (1479–1542), also known as Lisa Gherardini, and that it was commissioned by her husband, Francesco del Giocondo (1465–1542). The name *Mona Lisa* would have been shortened from Madonna Lisa, meaning my lady Lisa.

> **"I have heard it said that [the *Mona Lisa*] creates the illusion of life. It does much more; it creates the illusion of dreaming."**
>
> **JULIEN GREEN (1900–1998), *DIARIES***

One thing is certain—the *Mona Lisa* was never delivered to a client. Leonardo still had the painting with him when he died. Why he never finished the painting is also a mystery.

Clos Lucé, Leonardo's last home in France

credit: Itto Ogami

IN JAPAN

While Leonardo painted *The Last Supper* and the *Mona Lisa*, the Japanese artist Kano Masanobu (1434–1530) started a 300-year tradition in Japan known as the Kano School of Painting. Kano artists worked on large paintings that adorned the castle walls of Japanese rulers. Their most common subjects were birds, trees, flowers, animals, and dragons, which they painted with a landscape in the background. Like their counterparts in medieval and Renaissance Europe, the Japanese Kano painters favored gold leaf. This was especially the case when they painted on large folding screens or sets of sliding doors. Some of the best examples of Kano painting can be seen today at Nijo Castle in Kyoto, in the south of Japan.

A fan painting by Kano Motohide from the sixteenth century shows a view of Kyoto.

Trusted Companion

Like all Renaissance artists, Leonardo did not work alone. He always had numerous pupils and assistants. One such person was Francesco Melzi (1491–1568). Melzi was the son of a noble family from the Lombardy area of Italy. No one would have expected him to become an artist! But he became Leonardo's pupil when he was a teenager, and he became an artist in his own right when he was an adult.

Melzi stayed with Leonardo as an assistant and companion for the rest of Leonardo's life. After Leonardo died, it was Melzi who gained possession of his master's drawings and notebooks. We have Melzi to thank for saving these for posterity.

Portrait of Leonardo

By Francesco Melzi, after 1510

KINDNESS FOR ALL CREATURES

Leonardo had a reputation for gentleness and compassion. He extended his kindness not only to people, but to animals as well. People told stories of Leonardo buying caged birds on the streets of Florence just so he could set them free. And at some point as an adult, he became a vegetarian. He didn't want to kill a living creature to feed himself.

WONDER WHY?

Who supports artists today? Can you think of any modern-day patrons? Does government have a role in supporting artists?

Leonardo's Legacy

By the time he died of a stroke at age 67, Leonardo was almost forgotten in the world of Italian art. Leonardo was in Rome while Michelangelo and Raphael worked on important commissions for Pope Leo X (1475–1522) there, but had no important commissions himself.

WORDS OF WONDER

What vocabulary words did you discover? Can you figure out the meanings of these words by using the context and roots? Look in the glossary for help!

**bottega · guild · lavish
restoration · posterity**

The Garden of Earthly Delights
The triptych (three-paneled painting) by Hieronymus Bosch

NORTHERN RENAISSANCE

How far did Renaissance artists rebel against the traditions of medieval art? In the case of Netherlands artist Hieronymus Bosch (1450–1516), very far indeed! The theme of *The Garden of Earthly Delights* is religious, but the style is exuberantly unique. Can you describe everything that is going on in these paintings?

Leonardo's last patron was King Francis I of France. He provided Leonardo with a place to live and they became close friends during the last years of Leonardo's life.

No one overlooks Leonardo today. Even his unfinished works are considered masterpieces. In November 2017, an unfinished painting of Jesus attributed to Leonardo, *Salvator Mundi*, sold for more than $450 million at auction.

Minerva Dressing

Oil on canvas painting of a Roman goddess by Lavinia Fontana (1613)

Salvator Mundi

Attributed to Leonardo da Vinci, circa 1500, although many experts doubt it is actually by him

RENAISSANCE WOMEN

Most female Renaissance artists were trained by their fathers and most painted portraits more than anything else. Lavinia Fontana (1552–1614) was no exception. Unlike other female artists, however, Fontana also painted religious pictures and nudes. In fact, she was the first European female artist to ever paint a nude.

Fontana accepted commissions from some of the wealthiest and most powerful people in Italy, including at least two popes. She was the most prolific female artist of her time, and also one of the best paid. Her work supported a family of 13 people.

The Human Body in Art

Leonardo was one of several Renaissance artists who dissected human corpses. Why did they do that? To better understand the form and function of the human body, which they believed was created in the image of God. To them, the human body—inside and out—was a source of knowledge.

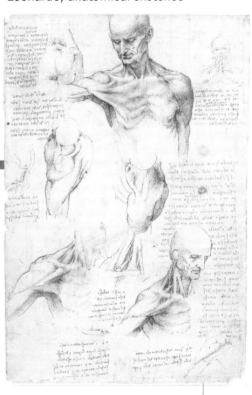

Leonardo, anatomical sketches

> **How do we feel about the human body today?** Do you know of any modern artists who glorify the human body in their art? Do you see many images of the human body in popular culture? If so, what kind of images do you see? What do they suggest about how we think about the human form?

> **Leonardo made some of the most accurate drawings of human anatomy of all time.** Choose one external human body part—an ear, a hand, a foot, for example— and make the most accurate drawing of it that you can. Use your own body as a model or work with a partner. If you prefer to write rather than draw, create a written description instead.

> **Which body part did you choose and why?** How hard was it to get the details right? What did you learn about that part of the body by having to study it so closely? Does a careful examination of the human body change your feelings about it? Why or why not?

CONNECT

Train your hand to draw what you see with a lesson on contour drawing.

🔍 **easy way contour drawing**

43

Compare and Contrast

The image of Saint John the Baptist shows up time and again in medieval and Renaissance art. But how this saint is depicted varies a great deal from artist to artist. Below are two versions of John the Baptist.

The painting on the left is by Verrocchio. It depicts a scene from the New Testament when Jesus allows John (on the right) to baptize him.

The painting on the right is a portrait of John by Leonardo.

Verrocchio, *The Baptism of Christ*

Leonardo, *St. John the Baptist*

Project

> **Write down or discuss with friends or classmates a description of Saint John from each of these paintings.** Consider these questions.

- What are the biggest differences between them?
- Do you find any similarities?
- What does each artist want to communicate about the character of Saint John?
- Is one painting more appealing than the other? Why or why not?

Try This!

Many Catholic saints make repeat appearances in Renaissance art. Along with Saint John, they include Saints Anne, Barnabas, Stephen, Catherine, Peter, Paul, Joseph, and Jerome.

> **Research and create a presentation of your own design about one of those saints.** Be sure to include the following information.

- Where and when they lived
- What they did to become a saint
- What special objects (if any) they are traditionally associated with
- How they have most often been represented in religious art

Portrait of Michelangelo
By Jacopino del Conte,
circa 1540

CHAPTER 3

Michelangelo

Michelangelo was not an easy guy to get along with. When he was a teenager, he made a classmate so angry, the boy punched Michelangelo in the face and broke his nose. As he grew older, his relationships didn't improve much. When he was an adult, he insulted the sweet-tempered Leonardo da Vinci on the streets of Florence. He accused artists of stealing commissions from him. He imagined people wanted to kill him.

Detail from *The Creation of Adam*
By Michelangelo, circa 1511

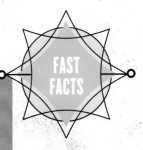

FAST FACTS

BIRTH DATE: 1475

PLACE OF BIRTH: CAPRESE, ITALY

AGE AT DEATH: 89

PLACE OF BURIAL: BASILICA OF SANTA CROCE, FLORENCE

FAMOUS ARTWORKS:
- *BACCHUS*
- *PIETÀ*
- *DAVID*
- SISTINE CHAPEL CEILING

> "He was so obsessed by drawing that he used to spend on it all the time he possibly could. As a result he used to be scolded . . . by his father and the older members of the family. . . ."
>
> **GIORGIO VASARI, *LIVES OF THE ARTISTS***

Yet when Michelangelo died, the people of Florence honored him with a funeral procession fit for a hero. Perhaps not everyone liked the man, but everyone respected the artist.

Early Years

Michelangelo di Lodovico Buonarroti Simoni was born in a small town called Caprese, near Arezzo, Tuscany. His father, Ludovico di Leonardo Buonarroti Simoni, was a town administrator there. When Michelangelo was several months old, the family moved to Florence, where the Simoni family had been bankers for generations.

Michelangelo's mother died when he was six years old. But even before she passed, she was frequently ill and unable to take care of him.

AMONG THE STONECUTTERS

As an adult, Michelangelo always said he learned his love of sculpting from his early childhood experiences. He was drawn to marble, and he became expert at spotting the best pieces to use for his sculptures. When possible, he quarried the marble himself—a difficult and dangerous job that most artists left to others. But Michelangelo felt at home among the stonecutters. Plus, he was a perfectionist. He wanted complete control over his work, from start to finish.

Michelangelo
1475–1564

1488
As a young man, he studies with Ghirlandaio.

1490
Michelangelo studies with Lorenzo de Medici.

1496
He moves to Rome and sculpts the fake cupid and *Bacchus*.

1498
He sculpts *Pietà* in Rome.

Male Nude, turning to the Right

Drawing by
Michelangelo, circa 1511

Michelangelo was sent to be looked after by a couple who lived in the nearby town of Settignano. The town was known for its marble quarries, and the husband was a stonecutter who worked in the quarries. Perhaps this was where Michelangelo first got a sense of the marble that would become his life's passion.

WONDER WHY?

How do parents feel about their children becoming artists today? Are artists respected? Do they make a lot of money?

1504
In Florence, Michelangelo completes *David* and begins, but does not finish, the *Battle of Cascina* fresco.

1512
He completes the ceiling of the Sistine Chapel.

1541
Michelangelo completes *The Last Judgment* in the Sistine Chapel.

1545
He completes sculptures for the tomb of Pope Julius II.

1547
In Rome, Michelangelo works as an architect on St. Peter's Basilica.

1564
Michelangelo dies in Rome.

Michelangelo's career got off to a rough start. When he told his father he wanted to be an artist, his father was not pleased. No son of his was going to be an artist!

Why would a Renaissance father not want his son to be an artist? In the 1400s, artists were not respected professionals. Their shops were often set up in the poorer parts of town, and the work itself could be dirty and dangerous. Certainly, artists were not regarded as geniuses. They were craftsmen who merely did as they were told by their patrons.

But Michelangelo's talent was undeniable. So when he was 13, his father set him up as an apprentice with Domenico Ghirlandaio (1449–1494).

Ghirlandaio was best known for his frescoes. Michelangelo stayed with Ghirlandaio for only a year, but he learned the art of fresco when he assisted Ghirlandaio with a series of murals in the Tornabuoni Chapel in Florence.

In the Medici Palace

While Michelangelo was an apprentice in Ghirlandaio's bottega, he caught the attention of Lorenzo de Medici (1449–1492). Known as *Il Magnifico*—"The Magnificent"—Lorenzo de Medici was the wealthiest, most powerful man in Florence. He was also a supporter of humanist thinkers and a great patron of the arts.

CONNECT

The Medici palace is now a museum. You can see some of the artwork at the museum's website.

🔍 **Medici Riccardi Palace**

Marriage of Mary
By Ghirlandaio, Michelangelo's first teacher

THE ART OF FRESCO

Frescoes are paintings made on plaster that has been freshly applied to a wall or ceiling and is still damp. It's an art form that calls for enormous skill and confidence. To make a fresco, you have to make and apply cartoons. These are full-scale drawings done on paper. When the plaster is still moist, the cartoon is nailed to the wall. Then, holes are pricked into the drawing, and a small cloth bag filled with charcoal dust is pounded over the holes so the charcoal goes through. This transfers the cartoon image to the wall. Only then can you start painting. The plaster and the paint dry quickly, and once they do, fixing mistakes is not easy. If you goof up, you have to start over—all new plaster, all new paint.

Courtyard of the Medici palace, Florence

credit: Gryffindor

Impressed with Michelangelo's talent, Lorenzo took the young man into his home. He treated him like an adopted son. In the Medici home, Michelangelo mixed with the leading humanists of Florence who gathered there to discuss literature, art, and philosophy.

Lorenzo had a sculpture garden where he displayed ancient Greek and Roman statues. From 1490 to 1492, Michelangelo spent a lot of time in Lorenzo's garden, studying and drawing those ancient works of art.

Rome and the Fake Cupid

Michelangelo moved to Rome in 1496. He was only 21, and not yet a well-known artist. To get himself noticed, he decided to sculpt a cupid and pass it off as an ancient work of art.

Humanist art collectors loved ancient sculptures. They believed that no living artist could make anything as beautiful as what the ancients had made.

To prove them wrong, Michelangelo sculpted a cupid and sold it to a collector, who believed he was buying an antique.

The customer was not happy when he learned he had been duped. But the trick worked in Michelangelo's favor. It proved he was as talented as the ancients.

The commissions started coming in.

> "Every block of stone has a statue inside it and it is the task of the sculptor to discover it."
>
> **MICHELANGELO**

WONDER WHY?

Is it true that artists need lots of time alone? What might be the creative benefits of limiting your interactions with other people? What might be the creative benefits of spending time with other people?

The Loner

Of all the great Renaissance artists, Michelangelo was the least sociable. He had a quick temper and always suspected other artists were stealing his ideas or copying his work. It wasn't possible for a Renaissance artist to work in complete isolation. Assistants or apprentices were always needed. But as much as he could, Michelangelo limited the number of people who had access to his work sites.

Michelangelo was most at home in the company of his assistants. Many of the people he hired stayed with him for long stretches of time. If they worked hard and were loyal, he rewarded them with kindness and generosity.

For example, when a long-time assistant named Urbino was dying, Michelangelo stayed by his side. After he died, Michelangelo supported Urbino's wife and two children.

Bacchus

The fake cupid attracted the interest of Cardinal di San Giorgio (1461–1521). He commissioned Michelangelo to create a sculpture of Bacchus, the Roman god of wine. The cardinal wanted a sculpture that was divine, something to be worshipped.

What Michelangelo gave him was a young boy who was obviously drunk.

Disgusted, the cardinal refused to take ownership of the statue. Michelangelo's *Bacchus* wound up in the sculpture garden of a banker named Jacopo Galli (dates unknown).

Bacchus
circa 1496

Building his Reputation

After the *Bacchus* scandal, Michelangelo was hired to carve a sculpture for a cardinal's tomb.

People often said that Michelangelo was arrogant. Even when he was young, he acted as if he were the greatest artist of them all.

He certainly was confident. The contract for this next important commission stated that he would create "the most beautiful marble that there is today in Rome, and that no other living master will do better." Michelangelo signed his name and went to work on the *Pietà*.

> "[It] is necessary that [he] who wishes to attend to studies of art flee company."
>
> **MICHELANGELO, IN A LETTER TO VASARI**

Pietà, 1498

The *Pietà* is a religious statue carved in 1498 from white marble. It is 5 feet 9 inches by 6 feet 5 inches. You can find it at St. Peter's Basilica in Rome, where it was commissioned by Cardinal Jean Bilhères de Lagraulas (1434–1499).

Like the Madonna, the *Pietà* is a recurring subject in Christian art. It shows the Virgin Mary holding and mourning the dead body of Jesus after he was crucified.

CONNECT

Have a lesson on the *Pietà*

🔍 **Khan Academy Pietà**

> **"It is certainly a miracle that a formless block of stone could ever have been reduced to a perfection that nature is scarcely able to create in the flesh."**
>
> GIORGIO VASARI, *LIVES OF THE ARTISTS*

From Rome to Florence

From the moment the *Pietà* was unveiled, people were astounded by the size, beauty, delicacy, and realism of Michelangelo's work. In the opinion of most people, Michelangelo had, indeed, lived up to the terms of his contract.

When Michelangelo returned to Florence in 1501, he arrived with his reputation firmly in place. And now, city leaders in Florence presented him with a great challenge. Thirty years earlier, they had purchased an enormous column of marble, intending it to become a sculpture to adorn the Florence Cathedral.

Two artists had already tried to make something out of it. Both had failed.

But Michelangelo was fearless. Once again, he staked his reputation on being able to accomplish something that no other living artist could do.

David is a white marble statue of a male nude. It is 17 feet high and weighs 12,500 pounds. It stands in the Accademia, a gallery in Florence.

David is a figure from the Old Testament. His people are at war. Among the enemy is a giant man named Goliath. Goliath challenges the Israelites to send out one man who can kill him. David, a shepherd boy, accepts the challenge. Armed with only his faith, five stones, and a sling, David takes out Goliath with a single shot.

Michelangelo shows David just before he confronts Goliath. He holds a sling on his left shoulder and a stone in his right hand. His eyes are sharp. His brow is furrowed. His neck muscles are tight. The veins on his right hand bulge.

Michelangelo modeled *David* after the sculptures of ancient Greece and Rome. Those artists glorified the human body, and Michelangelo does, too. For him, *David* is a vision of man as God intended him to be—perfect.

> **"What spirit is so empty and blind, that it cannot recognize the fact that the . . . skin is more beautiful than the garment with which it is clothed?"**
>
> **MICHELANGELO**

All the same, not everyone was comfortable with the full exposure of the male body. When *David* was first installed, city leaders covered *David's* private parts with a garland of 28 copper leaves.

David, 1504

WONDER WHY?

Do you think great art takes great courage to make? What role does confidence play in being successful in the arts?

Money Problems

Michelangelo became one of the best-paid artists of the Renaissance, yet he never seemed to have enough money. Why? Much of what he made went to support his extended family. Michelangelo provided financial assistance to everyone from his father to his four brothers to his nieces and nephews.

When he wasn't giving money to family members, he was giving it to the poor or to others he felt deserved a little help.

WHERE SHOULD IT GO?

Originally, *David* was going to be placed high up on an outside wall of the Florence Cathedral. By the time it was finished, however, the 6-ton sculpture was too heavy to be lifted to the top of the building, and city leaders wanted to display it in a more public place anyway. But where? They created a committee to settle the question. Among the committee members were some of the greatest names in Renaissance art, including Botticelli and Leonardo da Vinci. They decided *David* should stand outside the Palazzo Vecchio, the seat of city government. Today, a model of the original *David* stands outside the Palazzo Vecchio.

One of his most unusual charitable habits was to provide dowries to the daughters of noblemen who had fallen on hard times. Marriage was essentially the only "career" open to Renaissance women. The dowries Michelangelo gave made it possible for these young women to find husbands and secure a livelihood.

CONNECT

Check out *David* at the Accademia. Why do so many people travel to see this statue? What artwork being created today will be as highly regarded 500 years from now?

🔍 denniscallan Accademia

The Reluctant Painter and the Sistine Chapel

Michelangelo made his reputation as a sculptor. It was what he most liked to do. During the early 1500s, he was happily at work on a commission to create 40 sculptures for the tomb of Pope Julius II (1443–1513).

Palazzo Vecchio in Florence, Italy

Then, the pope decided that he wanted Michelangelo to paint the ceiling of the Sistine Chapel in Rome. Michelangelo spent the next four years working on wooden scaffolding more than 60 feet in the air. He painted looking up at a curved surface that covered more than 12,000 square feet.

"It is well with me only when I have a chisel in my hand."

MICHELANGELO

He painted in fresco, the most challenging kind of painting. It was a monumental undertaking—especially for a man who didn't like to paint!

The Sistine Chapel houses dozens of religious scenes commissioned by Pope Julius II and painted in 1508 to 1512 on a ceiling that measures 133 feet by 46 feet. Today, about 5 million people a year visit the Sistine Chapel to see the paintings.

Ceiling of the Sistine Chapel, 1508–1512

The main section of the Sistine Chapel ceiling is made up of nine panels. In groups of three, they illustrate stories from the Bible's Book of Genesis. Three panels are about God's creation of the world. Another three are about Adam and Eve. Three more are about Noah.

But that's only a small part of Michelangelo's creation. The ceiling is a collection of Christian images. There are more than 150 pictorial units and more than 150 human figures.

CONNECT

Learn more about the ceiling of the Sistine Chapel.

🔍 **Khan Academy Sistine Chapel**

Of all the images, God's creation of Adam is the most famous. You can know nothing about Renaissance art and still recognize the picture of God reaching out his hand to Adam.

The Creation of Adam, Sistine Chapel

"Without having seen the Sistine Chapel one can form no appreciable idea of what one man is capable of achieving."

JOHANN WOLFGANG VON GOETHE (1749–1832)

Michelangelo in Love

Michelangelo may have been a loner, but that did not stop him from falling madly in love. When he was in his mid-50s, he fell head over heels in love with Tommaso de Cavalieri (1509–1587), a handsome, 23-year-old man from a wealthy family.

As a devout Catholic, Michelangelo struggled to resist his romantic interests in men, which went against Church teachings. But he also poured out his heart to Cavalieri in dozens of poems. When Michelangelo's grandnephew published those poems in 1623, they were the first significant series of poems in any modern language in which one man expressed his love for another man.

The Fall of Phaeton, 1533
A print of the drawing by Michelangelo, which he gave as a present to Cavalieri

Woodblock print of *Hercules at the Crossroad* (1498)

ALBRECHT DÜRER

Albrecht Dürer (1471–1528) was a German artist who painted some of the first watercolor landscapes in Europe, wrote books about mathematics, and painted religious altarpieces. He is best known, however, for his highly detailed woodblock prints. What Michelangelo accomplished across the enormous space of the Sistine Chapel ceiling, Dürer did on small pieces of wood. *Hercules at the Crossroad* shows Dürer's humanist interests in mythology and the human form.

Personal Appearance

Michelangelo was famous for caring very little about material comforts. Friends and family members would report that his living quarters were those of a beggar. He worked himself to the point of exhaustion and ate just enough to sustain himself.

> **"Good painting is the kind that looks like sculpture."**
>
> **MICHELANGELO**

His clothes were shabby and he often slept in them. Once, he wore his boots for so many days in a row, some of his skin peeled off when he finally removed them.

RENAISSANCE WOMEN

Because Sofonisba Anguissola (1532–1625) was a woman, she was not allowed to study nude models or dissect cadavers to understand the human body. Leonardo and Michelangelo did both those things, and the results are evident in the detail they put into their work.

Anguissola turned her attention to making portraits, but with a difference. Rather than paint people in formal poses, she portrayed them in everyday settings.

As a court painter for the King of Spain for 14 years, however, Anguissola also painted many formal portraits. By the time she died, she was one of the most important portrait artists of the Renaissance.

Self-Portrait, 1554 (left), *The Chess Game,* 1555 (right)

By Sofonisba Anguissola

Michelangelo's Legacy

Michelangelo's sculpture of David and his paintings in the Sistine Chapel forever changed the direction of European art. His depictions of the human form reached a level of perfection never seen before.

His art is still a work of wonder today. Artists from around the world learn their craft by studying his techniques. And each year, millions of tourists stare up at the ceiling of the Sistine Chapel, stand in awe of *David*, and feel humbled by the beautiful *Pietà*.

It's exactly what the boy with the broken nose always wanted.

WORDS OF WONDER

What vocabulary words did you discover? Can you figure out the meanings of these words by using the context and roots? Look in the glossary for help!

procession · isolation
dowry · livelihood · typify

Bihzad, *The Seduction of Yusuf*, 1488

IN AFGHANISTAN

While Michelangelo was painting the ceiling of the Sistine Chapel, a Persian artist named Kamal al-din Bihzad (1450–1535) was painting some of the finest miniatures and illuminated manuscripts in all the Middle East. In Bihzad's work, you see the brilliant colors and recurring geometric patterns that typify much of Islamic art. His paintings also display a lot of action, such as work crews building walls or camels fighting while their owners try to pull them apart. One of his most famous paintings, *The Seduction of Yusuf*, shows a man leaping from a very high balcony.

Compare and Contrast

The man who commissioned the *Bacchus* from Michelangelo was not the only one who found it offensive. When the English poet Percy Bysshe Shelley (1792–1822) saw it hundreds of years later, he said it was "revolting."

➤ **Above are two statues of Bacchus.** One is by an unknown artist from 130 CE. The other is by Michelangelo.

· Can you tell which is which?

· Does one seem offensive to you, and the other acceptable? Why or why not?

· Which statue would you add to your sculpture garden?

· What do you look for in art—truth, beauty, social commentary, or something else?

ANSWER: left is unknown, right is Michelangelo

Collaborative Creations

Renaissance art was nearly always a group activity. The master artist may have been in charge, but he depended on assistants to perform numerous crucial tasks. Many times, assistants and apprentices even created parts of the artwork itself.

> **Consider these questions as you look at the art in this book.** Discuss them among your classmates or friends or respond to them in a journal entry.

- Does knowing this change your appreciation of Renaissance art?
- Do you see the work any differently when you imagine a group of people, rather than a lone artist, creating it together?

- Are Renaissance assistants and apprentices given enough credit for their contributions?
- Is it fair that only the master artist signs his name to a work of art that it took many hands to create?

Try This!

> **Form a group of three to four friends or classmates and create a work of collaborative art.** What you decide to make is up to the group. But be sure to choose a project that requires a true team effort.

> **When your project is done, consider these questions.**

- What was the hardest part about working on art as a group? What was the most fun?
- Did one person lead or was it a more democratic process?
- Were you able to express yourself artistically in the group?
- Are you pleased with what you created? Why or why not?
- Do you feel a sense of personal ownership of the artwork? Does it belong to you or does it belong to the group?

CONNECT

See one method of transferring a Renaissance cartoon.

🔍 **YouTube cartoon transfer process**

CHAPTER 4

Raphael

Dome of Santa Maria del Popolo, 1516

No other Renaissance artist rose to fame as quickly as Raphael. At an age when most artists were still apprentices, Raphael signed a major commission. In the contract, he was referred to as maestro, or "master." He was just 17 years old!

FAST FACTS

BIRTH DATE: 1483

PLACE OF BIRTH: URBINO, ITALY

AGE AT DEATH: 37

PLACE OF BURIAL: THE PANTHEON IN ROME

FAMOUS ARTWORKS:
- *THE MARRIAGE OF THE VIRGIN*
- *DONI PORTRAITS*
- *THE SISTINE MADONNA*
- *THE SCHOOL OF ATHENS*

By the time he was 21, Raphael was winning important commissions in Florence. A few years after that, he was working on frescoes for Pope Julius II in Rome. When Julius II saw Raphael's work, he not only fired a handful of other artists, he also instructed Raphael to paint over their work.

Climbing to the top of the Italian Renaissance art world was no small accomplishment. To get there required talent, of course. But art was also a business, and Raphael was one of the Renaissance's sharpest art businessmen.

Palazzo Ducale at Urbino

Raphael
1483–1520

1483
Raphael is born in Urbino to the artist Giovanni Santi.

1494
Raphael's father dies. Raphael continues the work of his father's studio.

1504
Raphael paints *The Marriage of the Virgin* and spends time in Florence.

1506
Raphael paints the portraits of Agnolo and Maddalena Doni.

Early Years

Raffaello Sanzio was the son of the artist and poet Giovanni Santi (1435–1494) and a woman named Margia. Santi was court painter for the Duke of Urbino, and he ran his bottega right next to the family home.

From the time Raphael could walk, he found his way into his father's studio. Soon enough, everyone realized that Giovanni's son was a promising young artist himself.

Raphael's childhood, however, was marked by tragedy. Before he was even 12 years old, he had survived the death of two siblings, his mother, a stepsister, and then his father.

He was left an orphan. Fortunately, he was cared for by two groups of people: his extended family and his father's assistants. Together, they nurtured Raphael's talent and set him up to take over his father's business.

The Virgin and Child
By Giovanni Santi, 1480s

1507
Influenced by Leonardo's work, he paints the *Madonna of the Pinks*.

1508
Raphael begins work on frescoes for the papal apartments.

1509–1511
He works on *The School of Athens*.

1512
Raphael paints a portrait of Pope Julius II and *The Sistine Madonna*.

1514
Raphael works as an architect for Pope Leo X.

1520
Raphael dies Rome of a fever.

Raphael's Teachers

Raphael's first and most important teacher was his father. Santi was an accomplished and innovative painter, especially respected for his portraits. Another key influence was his father's former assistant, a man named Evangelista (dates unknown). After Raphael's father died, it was Evangelista who furthered Raphael's education.

Raphael not only worked by Evangelista's side in the studio, he also accompanied Evangelista on his travels, meeting with patrons and hammering out contracts—learning the business side of art.

Did Raphael ever serve an actual apprenticeship? No one can say for sure. His early work certainly was influenced by the painter Pietro Perugino (1446–1523), a master artist 40 years older than Raphael. But no documents remain that prove Raphael was ever Perugino's student.

IN MEXICO

At about the time that Raphael was born, artists in the Mexican city of Calixtlahuaca (current day Mexico City) finished up work on a monumental sculpture known as the *Great Aztec Earth Goddess*. The statue stands nearly 8 feet tall and its Aztec name is *Coatlicue*, which roughly translates to "snakes-her-skirt." *Coatlicue* is imposing, solid, and composed of multiple images and figures, including a mass of snakes writhing around her lower half. To the Europeans who colonized the Aztec people, the statue of Coatlicue seemed monstrous and bizarre. To native Mexican Indians, however, *Coatlicue* was a goddess. They worshipped at her feet and honored her with candles and flowers.

Today, you can visit *Coatlicue* at the National Museum of Anthropology in Mexico City, Mexico.

Statue of Coatlicue from the back

map credit: Heraldry

WONDER WHY?

How did early exposure and access to art affect Raphael's life? Would he have succeeded without the help of his father and Evangelista? In addition to talent, what kind of help do young people need today in order to succeed in a profession?

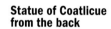

Outdoing a Master

Raphael built his early reputation in Città di Castello, a small town in central Italy near Perugia. That was Pietro Perugino's territory, where he had made his career. But as Raphael's star rose, Perugino's faded. That was especially the case when Raphael accepted a commission to paint *The Marriage of the Virgin*.

The wedding between Mary and Joseph was a common theme in Christian art. In fact, Perugino had made a *Marriage* painting only a few years before, in 1499.

> **"When one is painting one does not think."**
>
> **RAPHAEL**

When Raphael took up the subject in 1504, he closely modeled his *Marriage* on Perugino's work. But Raphael didn't simply copy Perugino's work. He improved on it in many ways. Take a look at the two paintings side-by-side.

Raphael, *The Marriage of the Virgin*, 1504

Perugino, *Marriage of the Virgin*, 1499

Both show Mary and Joseph being married by a priest in front of a temple. Both show Joseph putting a ring on Mary's finger. Both show a collection of people. Both show all the men (except the priest) holding narrow rods, with only Joseph's sprouting a plant. Both show one man breaking a rod over his knee.

> **"Poor is the pupil who does not surpass his master."**
>
> **LEONARDO DA VINCI**

But if you look closely, you'll see some key differences. Take another look and ask yourself these questions.

+ Which temple seems more detailed?

+ Which priest seems more realistic?

+ Which group seems more naturally posed?

+ Which painting has more natural looking shadows and light?

+ Which painting has the more appealing Virgin Mary?

CONNECT

Learn more about the wedding of Mary and Joseph.

🔍 **Khan Academy Marriage of Virgin**

When Renaissance patrons compared the work of the older master with that of the young upstart, they crowned Raphael the greater of the two artists. How do you think Perugino felt about that?

WONDER WHY?

How did connections to powerful people help Raphael in Florence? Did they give him an unfair advantage over other artists? Would talent alone have been enough to lift him above the competition? Why or why not?

Raphael's Next Move

Renaissance art was a competitive field. There were only so many wealthy patrons to go around, and artists competed to attract the most important and lucrative commissions. By directly taking on Perugino, Raphael had established himself as a force to be reckoned with in Umbria.

But Raphael had his sights set on bigger things.

In 1504, both Leonardo and Michelangelo were working in Florence. Leonardo was fresh off his success with *The Last Supper*. Michelangelo's *David* had just been installed outside the Florence city hall, the Palazzo Vecchio. And now, these two titans were both painting murals for the walls *inside* the Palazzo Vecchio. Leonardo's was *The Battle of Anghiari*. Michelangelo's was the *Battle of Cascina*.

Everyone in Florence was taking bets on which artist would create the more masterful work of art. This was not an opportunity Raphael could pass up.

> "Time is a vindictive bandit to steal the beauty of our former selves."
>
> **RAPHAEL**

Raphael's Introduction to Florence

Raphael was one of countless young artists who flocked to Florence to see what Leonardo and Michelangelo were up to. Indeed, so many curious artists got their hands on Michelangelo's cartoon drawings for the *Battle of Cascina* that they were nearly destroyed.

Luigi Schiavonetti (1765–1810), Engraved *Battle of Cascina*, after Michelangelo (top)

The Battle of Anghiari, copy of a detail after Leonardo (bottom)

ABANDONED ART

Neither Leonardo nor Michelangelo ever finished their famous battle scenes for the Palazzo Vecchio. In a failed experimental technique, Leonardo's fresco ran right off the wall. He never returned to the work again. Michelangelo drew the preparatory cartoons, then left them behind to work on a commission of 40 sculptures for Pope Julius II in Rome.

The Doni Portraits, 1506

Maddalena Doni (top) and Agnolo Doni (bottom)

Raphael, however, did not have to push through a crowd to get a closeup look at the great artists' work. He arrived in Florence with a letter of introduction from an influential patron back in Umbria. And the highest civic leader in Florence, Piero Soderini (1452–1522), made it known that Raphael should be warmly welcomed.

Soderini controlled the money for many art commissions in Florence. To please Soderini, Leonardo and Michelangelo invited Raphael into their homes and work places.

> **"Pictures painted by Raphael are truth itself: for in his figures the flesh seems to be moving, they breathe, their pulses beat, and they are utterly true to life."**
>
> **GIORGIO VASARI, *LIVES OF THE ARTISTS***

Learning from Leonardo

While Raphael was in Florence, he studied Leonardo's work and then adapted what he learned to his own art. This was especially evident in the area of portraiture.

Raphael got a close look at Leonardo's unfinished *Mona Lisa*. Within two years, he painted a set of portraits that made his reputation in Florence—and clearly showed Leonardo's influence on his work.

The 1506 portraits of Agnolo and Maddalena Doni (dates unknown) are oil on wood. Each measures 18 inches by 25 inches. The portraits were commissioned by Agnolo Doni and were originally displayed in the Doni home. They now hang in the Palazzo Pitti in Florence.

CONNECT

Listen to a discussion of the similarities and differences between the *Mona Lisa* and *Maddalena* at this website.

🔍 **Mona Lisa and Raphael's Maddalena**

Can you see how Raphael's portraits of Agnolo and Maddalena Doni owe an artistic debt to the *Mona Lisa*? The similarities are there, especially in the three-quarter poses of the subjects and the inclusion of a landscape for a background. Those were Leonardo's innovations, which Raphael copied but also made uniquely his own.

What did people admire most about the Doni portraits? They were drawn to Raphael's attention to detail, whether in a wisp of hair or in a decorative button. They loved the velvety richness of the Donis' clothes and the calm, light-infused landscape in the background.

THE AMOROUS MAN

The Renaissance art historian Giorgio Vasari once described Raphael as a "very amorous man." He meant that Raphael had numerous romantic relations with many women. At least two women, however, were special. One was Maria Bibbiena (dates unknown), a young woman to whom Raphael was engaged for more than five years before she died in 1520. The other was Margherita Luti (1500–1522), the daughter of a Roman baker. Margherita was the subject of at least two paintings. In his will, Raphael left an inheritance to Margherita so that she would be cared for after his death.

Raphael, *La Donna Velata*
Portrait of Margherita Luti, 1516

But more than anything else, they loved the feeling that Agnolo and Maddalena were actually *there*. Raphael had not only captured their appearance, he had captured their inner personalities. He had made them come alive on a piece of wood.

Learning from Michelangelo

What did Raphael take away from Michelangelo? The beauty, power, and expressiveness of the human body!

In a Madonna known as the *Doni Tondo*, Michelangelo depicted the Virgin Mary in a highly naturalistic and contorted pose. The figure represented a new accomplishment in Renaissance art, and Raphael incorporated it into a painting called the *The Deposition*.

> **"Everything [Raphael] knew about art he got from me."**
> **MICHELANGELO**

Take a look at Michelangelo's *Doni Tondo* Madonna. Then, look at the kneeling female figure twisting around to hold up a fainting woman in the right corner of Raphael's *The Deposition*. Do you see any similarities?

Tondo is an Italian art term that refers to a round painting or relief. When you see the word "tondo" in the title for a work of art, you know it's going to be round.

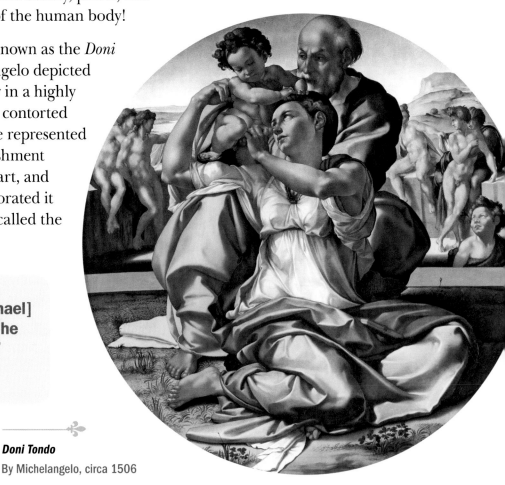

Doni Tondo
By Michelangelo, circa 1506

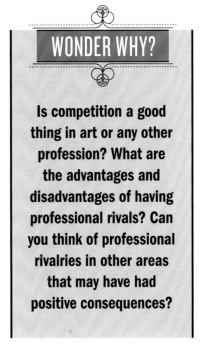

WONDER WHY?

Is competition a good thing in art or any other profession? What are the advantages and disadvantages of having professional rivals? Can you think of professional rivalries in other areas that may have had positive consequences?

The Deposition
By Raphael, 1507

Next, the Vatican

With his reputation in Florence confirmed, Raphael looked to Rome for more fame and fortune. In 1509, Pope Julius II was bringing artists from all over Italy to beautify the Holy City and to immortalize his own name with dozens of sculptures for his eventual tomb.

Any artist with ambition wanted a commission from Julius II. Armed with another letter of introduction from a loyal patron in Urbino, that's exactly what Raphael sought.

He arrived in Rome when he was just 25 years old and was given one of the most important jobs—decorating the pope's living quarters at the Vatican.

Raphael's assignment was to decorate the walls in Pope Julius II's apartment. In one room, the pope's library (later called the Stanza della Segnatura or Room of the Segnatura), Raphael did something truly unusual. He brought under one roof both the religious and secular interests of the Renaissance period.

On one wall of the Stanza della Segnatura, Raphael painted a religious scene. On the second, he developed a theme of poetry and art. On the third, he looked at six human virtues. On the last, he explored philosophy.

As a group, the four paintings represented much of what educated Renaissance men and women were eager to understand—religion, art, human virtue, and knowledge.

The School of Athens

Of the four frescoes in the Stanza della Segnatura, *The School of Athens* is the most well known. It is admired for its thematic importance, its balanced composition, and the beautiful, soft light that shines throughout the painting.

The School of Athens, 1511

A fresco on a wall, 25 feet 3 inches by 16 feet 5 inches

WORDS OF WONDER

What vocabulary words did you discover? Can you figure out the meanings of these words by using the context and roots? Look in the glossary for help!

virtue · tondo · adapt · debt · titan

The School of Athens is located in the Stanza della Segnatura at the Vatican Palace in Rome. In this painting, a crowd is gathered in a grand room that is filled with light. At the center and toward the back are two men. The man in red holds a book and points to the sky. The man in blue holds a book and motions to the immediate area. All around, people are engaged in various forms of study and conversation.

In *The School of Athens*, Raphael brings together some of the most important thinkers of the ancient world. The man in red is Plato, pointing to the heavens, or the spiritual world. The man in blue is Aristotle, pointing to the ground, or the known world. And the others? Historians have debated that question for centuries!

CONNECT

Take a virtual tour of the Stanza della Segnatura.

🔍 **Raphael Athens Khan**

Raphael himself never identified the ancient philosophers in this painting. An educated guess, however, suggests the following individuals: Epicurus, Pythagoras, Socrates, Heraclitus, Diogenes, Euclid, Archimedes, Ptolemy, and Apelles.

Still Life
By Fede Galizia, circa 1610

RENAISSANCE WOMEN

Fede Galizia (1578–1630) followed in the footsteps of her artist father, Nunzio Galizia, and became a portraitist. She lived in Milan, Italy. At age 12, when most artists are just beginning their training, she was already an accomplished artist. Her portraits were highly regarded for their attention to realistic detail in clothing and jewelry. But she was more influential as a still life painter. A still life painting is a detailed depiction of common objects, such as flowers or fruit. In that genre, she was a pioneer for all—men and women alike—who came after her.

People have also tried to figure out which Renaissance men Raphael used as models for this work. It's fairly certain that Plato is modeled after Leonardo da Vinci. Heraclitus—the bearded man resting his head on his hand—is modeled after Michelangelo.

The painting also includes a self-portrait! Raphael is wearing a black cap among a group of four men at the far right.

Sistine Madonna

Raphael painted dozens of variations of the Virgin Mary and the baby Jesus. Patrons admired how naturalistic they were. All the love and tenderness that exist between Mary and her child shine through in Raphael's Madonnas.

One of Raphael's most famous Madonnas was commissioned by Pope Julius II for a church in Piacenza in 1512.

The painting is graceful, majestic, and playful. The two little cherubs gazing up at Mary from the bottom of the painting are two of the most recognizable figures in Western art. Do you recognize them?

The Sistine Madonna, **1512**

Oil on canvas, 8 feet 8 inches by 6 feet 5 inches

Life and Death in Rome

Raphael spent the last 12 years of his life in Rome. Young, successful, and outgoing, he dressed in the finest clothes, lived in grand houses, and surrounded himself with companions. He maintained one of the largest workshops of the Renaissance period, and his assistants became like members of his family. He left instructions in his will to divide his belongings among two long-time assistants after his death.

Raphael was much admired by the citizens of Rome. When he died, thousands of people came out to honor him at his funeral procession.

Raphael's Legacy

For centuries, the name of Raphael has been associated with beauty and grace in visual art. But in the 1800s, Raphael's name was also adopted by a group of English artists who started a movement known as the Pre-Raphaelite Brotherhood (PRB).

> "You will not hear talk about anything except the death of Raphael of Urbino, who died last night . . . leaving this court in a profound . . . state of sadness due to the fact that the great achievements that were expected of him will not now come about."
>
> **PANDOLFO PICO IN A LETTER TO ISABELLA D'ESTE**

Their movement, however, had more to do with reactions to Renaissance art in general than Raphael specifically. Tired of living in the shadows of the Renaissance masters, the Pre-Raphaelite artists longed to branch out in new directions. Their art combined elements of both medieval and Renaissance art with a unique modern sensibility.

The Girlhood of Mary Virgin

Rossetti, 1818. First painting to include the initials PRB

Compare and Contrast

Raphael was adept at incorporating other artists' ideas and techniques into his work while creating something uniquely his own. Here are two similarly posed Madonnas.

Leonardo, *Benois Madonna* (1478)

➤ **List all the ways that Raphael's painting is like Leonardo's.** Then list all the ways that it is different. When you're done, consider the following questions.

· Do you like one Madonna more than the other? Why or why not?

· Does one of these Madonnas seem less Renaissance and more modern? Why or why not?

· Did Raphael copy Leonardo's work? And if he didn't copy it, then what did he do?

· Did Raphael "improve" on Leonardo's *Benois Madonna* in the same way that he "improved" on Perugino's *Marriage of the Virgin*?

· People talk about art being "original." Is Raphael's Madonna original? Why should that be important?

➤ **Imagine or make your own Madonna.**

· What will it look like? Where and how will you pose the figures?

· What will the poses and location communicate about modern times?

· What will they express about religion or the relationship between mother and child?

Raphael, *Madonna of the Pinks* (1507)

The School of Athens

In *The School of Athens*, Raphael brought together some of the most important figures of the ancient world. Let's find out a little bit about who those people were.

> ➤ **Choose three or four names from the list below and do some research on them using the internet or the library.**

· Plato	· Ptolemy	· Heraclitus	· Archimedes
· Aristotle	· Pythagoras	· Diogenes	· Ptolemy
· Epicurus	· Socrates	· Euclid	· Apelles

> ➤ **Create a presentation that describes who these people were, where they came from, when they lived, and what kind of contribution they made to humankind.**

Try This!

> ➤ **Make or imagine a new *School of Athens*, one that reflects the most influential people of the twentieth and twenty-first centuries, from 1900 to the present.** Choose five to 10 people for your artwork.

- Who does your *School of Athens* include and why?

- Does it include only people who have had a positive impact, or also include people who have had a negative impact?

- Which professions does your *School of Athens* represent?

- Is it made up of both men and women, people of color, people from all around the world?

- In the end, how different is your *School of Athens* from Raphael's?

Self-portrait of Titian,
circa 1550–1562

CHAPTER 5

Titian

For decades, the cities of Florence, Rome, and Milan dominated the Italian art scene. Leonardo, Michelangelo, and Raphael set the standards by which other artists were measured. Then, Tiziano Vecellio, the man we know as Titian, came along. Suddenly, Venice was also on the map.

St. John the Evangelist,
circa early 1500s

BIRTH DATE: 1488

PLACE OF BIRTH:
CADORE, ITALY

AGE AT DEATH: 95

PLACE OF BURIAL:
SANTA MARIA GLORIOSA IN VENICE

FAMOUS ARTWORKS:
- *ASSUMPTION OF THE VIRGIN*
- *PESARO MADONNA*
- *BACCHUS AND ARIADNE*
- *VENUS OF URBINO*

Cadore, Italy

Photograph by
Antonio De Lorenzo
and Marina Ventayol

With Titian, Venice laid claim to one of the most versatile and innovative of all the Italian Renaissance painters. He produced an estimated 400 works of art, in subjects that ranged from religion to myth, from portraits to nudes to landscapes. People marveled at the intensity of Titian's colors and the boldness of his brushwork—just two aspects of his talent that have inspired art lovers for centuries.

Titian
1452–1519

1488
Tiziano Vecellio, later known as Titian, is born in Cadore, Italy.

1500
Titian begins his apprenticeship in Venice with Sebastian Zuccato.

1501
Titian begins his apprenticeship with the Bellini brothers.

1507
He collaborates with Giorgione on exterior frescoes for a merchants' warehouse in Venice.

1516
He paints the *Assumption of the Virgin* for Santa Maria Gloriosa in Venice.

Early Years

Titian was born in the mountainous northern Italian village of Cadore, near the border with Germany. He came from a well-established family with ties to nobility. Many relatives were lawyers, and Titian's father was himself a respected councilor, soldier, and manager of local mines.

No one knows how Titian's parents, Gregorio and Lucia, became aware of their son's artistic abilities. Stories have been told of a young Titian roaming the countryside, making pigments from the petals of flowers and drawing on rocks.

But that's a tale we hear about dozens of artists, so it may or may not be true.

What's known is that when Titian was 12, both he and his brother, Francesco, joined an uncle who lived in Venice. That's where Titian's training as an artist began.

THE FLOATING CITY

Located on a lagoon off the Adriatic Sea, Venice is one of the most unique cities in the world. Made up of 118 small islands, Venice is a town that floats on water. Buildings sit atop foundations of wooden piles driven down through mud and water until they reach a hard layer of compressed clay. Canals are Venice's roadways, gondolas are the city's taxis.

1523
Titian paints *Bacchus and Ariadne.*

1526
Titian paints *Pesaro Madonna,* also for Santa Maria Gloriosa.

1534
He completes the *Venus of Urbino.*

1548
Titian paints *Equestrian Portrait of Charles V.*

1553–1559
He works on *Poesie,* a series of mythologies for Philip II of Spain.

1576
Titian dies of plague in Venice.

85

Titian's Teachers

Titan learned his craft from three men. The first was Sebastian Zuccato (dates unknown), an artist who taught Titian basic skills. Within a year, Titian transferred to the studios of two brothers, Gentile Bellini (1429–1507) and Giovanni Bellini (1430–1516).

Gentile and Giovanni were both prominent artists, but it was the younger brother, Giovanni, who most influenced Titian's career. Unlike Gentile, Giovanni had mastered the ability to create the illusion of realistic depth in his paintings. And the physical realism and emotional power of his portraits had made him the most sought-after portraitist in Venice.

Titian absorbed Giovanni's skills into his own art, and then surpassed his master in almost every respect.

Titian and Giorgione

In the early years of his career, Titian assisted—and collaborated with—an innovative artist named Giorgione (1478–1510). The two worked so closely together, it was sometimes difficult to tell one man's work from the other. Even today, art historians debate whether some works should be attributed to Titian or to Giorgione.

Portrait of Doge Leonardo Loredan
By Giovanni Bellini, after 1501

"Art is stronger than Nature."

TITIAN

Giorgione died at a young age, so he did not produce a large body of art. Still, his work inspired not just Titian but many other artists as well.

His most famous painting, *The Tempest*, challenged traditional practices by not being based on a known story or person, such as the birth of Christ. When you look at *The Tempest*, you don't know its back story. The meaning of the painting becomes wide open to interpretation.

The Tempest
By Giorgione, 1506

CONNECT

Watch Sister Wendy discuss the art of Venice and the works of Giovanni Bellini, Titian, and Giorgione.

🔍 **Sister Wendy Venice**

WONDER WHY?

Do you prefer art that is about something specific, or do you prefer art that is more open-ended? Is one style of art better than another? Or is it only a matter of personal preference?

In the Public Eye

By the time Titian was 30 years old, he was focused almost entirely on furthering his career. He had yet to marry or to have any children, and the bulk of his income came from commissions for art that was displayed in private homes. As a result, the general public knew little about his work.

Equestrian Portrait of Charles V, 1548 (left)
A Man with a Quilted Sleeve, 1510 (right)

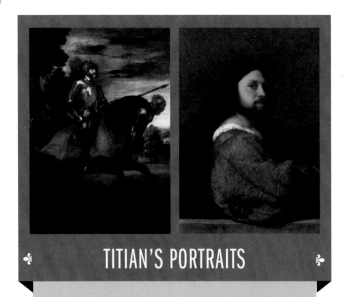

TITIAN'S PORTRAITS

Titian painted an estimated 100 portraits. Some of his subjects are difficult to identify, such as the mystery man in his celebrated *A Man with a Quilted Sleeve*. But many of Titian's portraits were of well-known public figures, such as his equestrian portrait of Charles V of Germany (1500–1558) and of Pope Paul II (1417–1471). Titian's portraits have long been admired for their psychological insight and their striking likeness to the people he painted.

That changed in 1518, when Titian completed his *Assumption of the Virgin* for the church of Santa Maria Gloriosa. It was the largest altarpiece in the city of Venice and, when it was unveiled, it caused a sensation. The intense colors and the energetic posing of the larger-than-life figures left viewers in awe, as well as a bit unsettled.

At first, many Venetians were not sure if they actually liked it. Soon enough, though, most people decided that Venice was now home to an artistic genius.

> "There was almost no famous lord, nor prince, nor great woman, who was not painted by Titian." "
>
> **GIORGIO VASARI, *LIVES OF THE ARTISTS***

The *Assumption of the Virgin* is an oil painting on a wood panel altarpiece that measures 11 feet 10 inches by 22 feet 8 inches. It was commissioned by the friars of Santa Maria Gloriosa in Venice and completed in 1518 at Santa Maria Gloriosa.

The *Assumption of the Virgin* captures the moment when God lifts the mother of Jesus from Earth directly into heaven. It is not just her soul, but her physical body, that is going to heaven.

Titian divides this scene into three parts—on the bottom are the 12 apostles, in the middle, Mary is surrounded by angels, and at the top is God. The angel on God's right holds a crown that will be placed on Mary's head.

What makes Titian's *Assumption* special? Before Titian, the standard interpretation of the Assumption was a scene of near absolute peace. In Giovanni Bellini's Assumption, for example, everyone stands still. Mary is calm. The apostles are not surprised by what's happening.

Assumption of the Virgin, 1516–18

WONDER WHY?

Why would Venetians want to say that their city had produced a great artist? Do modern cities like to boast about certain things? If so, what?

Titian, by contrast, portrays people actually reacting to the miracle. Everyone is swept up in the confusion of the moment. Fear and surprise are the emotional themes of his vision.

Virgin in Glory with Saints
By Giovanni Bellini, 1515

Life, Death, and Art

In 1526, Titian returned to Santa Maria Gloriosa for another groundbreaking commission. By then, however, his life had changed a great deal. He had married Cecilia, a young woman from his home village of Cadore, and together they had two sons—Pomponio and Orazio. But those happy events were intermixed with troubles. Cecilia and Titian endured the death of an infant daughter, and in 1525 Cecilia became so ill that she nearly died as well.

Poised between life and death, Titian painted a religious masterpiece—the *Pesaro Madonna.* Commissioned by Jacopo Pesaro (c. 1460–1547), the *Pesaro Madonna* is now in a chapel in Santa Maria Gloriosa in Venice.

In the *Pesaro Madonna*, Titian shook up the traditional composition of Madonna paintings. Composition in art is the placement of people and things in the scene.

CONNECT

Learn about the *Assumption of the Virgin*

🔍 **Khan Academy Assumption of Virgin**

Pesaro Madonna, 1519 to 1526

Oil on canvas, 8 feet 8 inches by 16 feet

For centuries, even artists as innovative as Giorgione followed an unwritten rule about the Madonna. Without fail, Mary and the baby Jesus were placed in the center of the painting.

Titian rewrote the rules to create a more visually engaging painting and to accommodate the viewpoints of people in different places in the church. He put Mary and Jesus up and to the right of the action and grouped figures along diagonal planes.

Mary and Jesus are still central to the theme, and even appear to be in the center to those walking down the aisle of the church. But now your eyes naturally roam from one grouping of people to the next. Your attention does not become fixated on one spot at the center.

The Luxury of Art

Throughout the Renaissance, religious works, portraits, and landscapes were displayed in public. Mythologies and nudes were displayed in private homes. Public or private, though, art was a luxury that few could afford. It was one way rich people displayed their wealth.

Titian's long career produced art for some of the wealthiest and most powerful people in Europe. His clients included kings and princes, dukes and duchesses, noblewomen and popes.

One such customer was Alfonso d'Este (1476–1535), the Duke of Ferrara. A rich man with an interest in mythology, d'Este hired artists to decorate his home with lavish illustrations of Greek and Roman myths. He commissioned Titian to paint what became one of his most celebrated mythologies—*Bacchus and Ariadne.*

Bacchus and Ariadne was originally housed in a private home. It now hangs in the National Gallery in London with two other works by Titian.

IN RUSSIA

The tradition of icon painting continued much longer in Russia than it did in other parts of Europe. But in Russia, it also developed into a far more elaborate and less religious form of art. Sometime in the late 1500s, a Russian artist known as Athanasius created one of the largest and most complex works of iconography in the world. Measuring more than 12 feet across and nearly 5 feet tall, the painting is a detailed depiction of a famous war victory by the ruler Ivan IV (also known as Ivan the Terrible) of Russia (1530–1584). Known as the *Church Militant*, or *Blessed Be the Host of the Heavenly Tsar*, the painting today is displayed in the Tretyakov Gallery in Moscow, Russia.

Church Militant, mid-sixteenth century

WONDER WHY?

Is art still a luxury item? Is it made only for wealthy people, or is it something that everyone can enjoy?

Bacchus and Ariadne, 1520–1523

Oil on canvas, 6 feet 9 inches by 5 feet 9 inches

"A good painter needs only three colors: black, white, and red."

TITIAN

In the ancient Greek myth, Ariadne was a princess who arrived on the island of Naxos with her boyfriend, Theseus. When she fell asleep, Theseus left without her.

In *Bacchus and Ariadne,* Titian captures the moment when Ariadne sees Theseus's ship in the distance and when Bacchus falls in love with her. Bacchus leaps from a chariot pulled by cheetahs.

He is accompanied by a group of fantastical partygoers. A circle of stars in the sky represent Ariadne's crown, which Bacchus has turned into a constellation.

Art critics have called this painting the greatest depiction of love at first sight. Why do you think they say that? Do you see an expression of sudden and powerful emotion in this painting? If not, what would you say is the theme of this painting?

Titian's Blended Family

Titian's first wife, Cecilia, died in 1530, leaving Titian to manage a demanding career while raising two young sons alone. Fortunately, his sister Orsa moved from Cadore to Venice and took charge of both the children and Titian's home.

Titian married again, but so little is known about his second wife we cannot even say for certain that his daughter, Lavinia, was her child. A fourth daughter, Emilia, was born to a woman with whom Titian had an affair.

THE VENETIAN STYLE

Venetian artists developed a style of painting that was quite different from the Florentine approach to art. The basis for Florentine art was drawing. Florence artists created detailed drawings to which color—in tempera or oil—was applied. Working with oil paints, Venetian artists frequently skipped the drawing step. They painted directly on the wood panel or canvas. The result was a style of painting that was often more impressionistic than that of Florence. The Venetian style is most apparent in Titian's later works. Viewed up close, the images in those paintings may blur. Viewed at a distance, they come into focus.

Son, Assistant, Artist

Orazio Vecellio (1528–1576) was the younger of Titian's sons. He served an apprenticeship under his father and then remained in his studio as an assistant. He developed an art career of his own, most recognized as a portrait artist, but he also accepted commissions for paintings of historical subjects. Before he died, he turned his professional attentions from art to chemistry. Orazio only lived to the age of 48. He and his father died of plague in the same year.

Titian, *An Allegory of Prudence*
(from left, Titian, Orazio, and Titian's nephew Marco Vecellio, circa 1550–circa 1565

RENAISSANCE WOMEN

Born at the tail end of the Renaissance, Artemisia Gentileschi (1593–1653) became one of the most accomplished and influential artists of Italy. Artemisia was trained by her father in Rome, but her work was far more influenced by the realism and innovative use of light seen in works by Caravaggio (1521–1610). Artemisia's most famous painting is *Judith Slaying Holofernes*, which she painted when she lived in Florence. It is remarkable for its realistic portrayal of a murder being committed by two women. Admired by her fellow artists in Florence, Artemisia was the first woman elected to the Florentine Academy of the Arts of Drawing.

What vocabulary words did you discover? Can you figure out the meanings of these words by using the context and roots? Look in the glossary for help!

versatile · contrast · Impressionistic composition · linear

Titian's Legacy

Throughout his long life, Titian remained attached to his hometown. He rarely left Venice, and when he did, it was usually to return to Cadore.

It's unfortunate then, that his death from the plague in 1576 prevented him from being buried in Cadore. His body was buried quickly in Venice to prevent the spread of the deadly disease.

Titian had a career that lasted for more than six decades, and he left behind a vast body of work. To understand the full scope of his many accomplishments is a daunting task. But it was his unique development of a less linear style of painting that perhaps had the greatest impact on the course of Western art.

Artemisia Gentileschi

Judith Slaying Holofernes, 1614–1620 (top); *Self-Portrait as the Allegory of Painting*, 1638–1639 (below)

Compare and Contrast

Below are two Renaissance paintings. One is a line-drawn painting by Botticelli. The other is a more color-based painting by Titian.

> **Can you tell which painting belongs to which artist?** Titian's use of color and his brushwork were innovations. But were they only improvements or a change? Are there improvements in art or are there only changes? Why or why not?

Try This!

> **Create a lightly sketched drawing and make two painted versions of the drawing.** In one, paint the drawing within the original lines. In the other, create the same picture on a blank piece of paper using only your paints.

· Which painting technique did you prefer?

· Did one feel more "artistic" than the other?

· Did one technique feel more expressive than the other? Why or why not?

ANSWER: left is Titian, right is Botticelli

Patronage and Public Art

Renaissance patrons played a direct role in the development of public art. They told artists what they wanted to adorn churches and government buildings that were open to the public. As a result, ordinary Renaissance citizens enjoyed access to some of the greatest Western art ever created.

➤ **By what means does public art come into existence today?**

➤ **Research the story behind a work of public art and create a presentation about what it is and how it came to be.** Your presentation should answer the following questions.

- Who commissioned the art?
- Was the work commissioned with a civic purpose in mind?
- Who paid for it? How was the artist chosen?
- Has the art ever been the subject of public debate?

CONNECT

Check out this TED Talk about the role of public art in a community. Do you think public art is important? Why or why not? Is there art where you live that everyone can look at?

 **TED Talk public art**

Try This!

➤ **Pretend that you are a wealthy patron who has the freedom to commission works of public art for the town where you live.** What kind of art would you choose? Where would you put it? Would it communicate a religious or secular message? What concerns among the public might you have to consider in your decision-making?

adapt: to make a change in response to new or different conditions.

adept: highly skilled.

adorn: to decorate something.

amorous: in love.

antiquity: something from ancient times.

apostles: Jesus's 12 original disciples in Christianity.

appreciable: capable of being weighed or appraised.

apprentice: a person who learns a job or skill by working for someone who is good at it.

apprenticeship: a time period in which a person is employed in order to learn a trade.

architecture: the style or look of a building.

arrogant: having an exaggerated sense of one's own importance or abilities.

attributed: a unique feature or characteristic.

basilica: a public building used as a courthouse or gathering hall in Rome.

BCE: put after a date, BCE stands for Before Common Era and counts down to zero. CE stands for Common Era and counts up from zero. These non-religious terms correspond to BC and AD. This book was printed in 2018 CE.

bottega: the studio or workshop of a major artist.

cadaver: a dead body.

cartoon: an initial drawing or design for a work of art, often a fresco.

cathedral: a large, important church.

charity: an act of aid to the needy.

chastity: abstaining from all sexual intercourse.

cherub: a childlike angel with wings.

Christian: a person who follows the religion of Christianity. Its central belief is that Jesus Christ is the son of God.

city-state: a city and its surrounding area, which rules itself like a country.

civic: relating to duty and responsibility to community.

civilization: a community of people that is advanced in art, science, and government.

classical: of or relating to the ancient Greek and Roman world.

collaborative: working together with other people.

commission: a legal contract for a work of art.

composition: in art, where and how things are placed in a painting or sculpture.

constellation: a group of stars that form a recognizable shape or pattern.

constraint: something that binds or holds back.

contort: to twist into strange shapes.

contrast: a relationship that focuses on the differences rather than the similarities.

convent: a community of people devoted to religious life and usually living together. Often nuns live in a convent.

corpse: a dead body.

counterpart: a corresponding part of a whole.

crucified: to put to death by nailing or binding the hands and feet to a cross.

culture: the beliefs and way of life of a group of people, which can include religion, language, art, clothing, food, holidays, and more.

cupid: a naked usually winged infantile figure representing the god of love.

debt: a service or money owed.

diplomat: a person who represents one country to another.

dissect: to cut something apart to study what's inside.

diverse: a large variety.

divine: belonging to God, or being godly.

dowry: the money, goods, or estate that a woman brings to her husband in marriage.

economy: the system of making and exchanging things of value and the wealth and resources of a country.

elaborate: very detailed and arranged.

embellished: lavishly decorated.

equestrian: relating to horseback riding.

era: a period of history marked by distinctive people or events.

exasperated: irritated or annoyed.

exuberant: filled with energy and excitement.

exude: to display an emotion or quality strongly.

Florentine: a native or resident of Florence, Italy.

fresco: a work of art painted with pigment on wet plaster on a wall or ceiling.

friar: a man employed by the Catholic Church.

genre: a category of artistic work.

gold leaf: a very thin sheet of gold.

goldsmith: an artisan who works with gold.

gondola: a flat-bottomed boat used on canals in Venice, Italy.

guild: a labor organization.

harbinger: a person sent ahead to announce the coming of someone.

homosexual: a person who is sexually attracted to others of the same gender.

humanism: a belief that human beings can improve themselves and their world through a rational approach to problem-solving.

humanist: a person who studies or supports humanism.

icon: a symbolic work of religious art.

iconography: pictures and other visual representations illustrating a subject, often of religious nature.

illegitimate: born of parents not married to each other.

immortalize: to be remembered forever.

impressionistic: in the style of impressionism, a style of art that gives a general view of something instead of particular detail.

infinite: with no limit, going on forever.

influential: having a strong effect on another person.

infuse: to introduce or suggest.

innovation: a new creation or a unique solution to a problem.

isolation: living separate from others.

lagoon: a shallow channel of water.

lavish: an abundance, more than what people expect.

linear: of or relating to a line.

literature: written work such as poems, plays, and novels.

livelihood: a source of income.

lucrative: something that is profitable, that makes money.

magi: a member of a priestly caste of ancient Persia.

mathematics: the study of math.

medieval: the Middle Ages, after the fall of the Roman Empire, from about 350 to 1450 CE.

Middle Ages: the period between the end of the Roman Empire and the beginning of the Renaissance, from about 350 to 1450 CE. It is also called the Medieval Era.

military engineer: someone who designs weaponry.

modest: not showing much of a person's body.

monk: a member of a religious community.

morally: from the point of view of right and wrong action or good and bad character.

mural: artwork painted directly on a wall, ceiling, or other large, permanent surface.

mythology: a collection of stories that are often focused on historical events. Myths express the beliefs and values of a group of people.

Nativity: birth, often refers to the birth of Jesus in Christianity.

naturalistic: looking and feeling natural.

nudity: the state of being naked.

patron: a person who gives financial support to a person or organization.

Persian: being from Persia, located in today's Iran.

philosophy: the study of truth, wisdom, the nature of reality, and knowledge.

pigment: a substance that gives something its color.

pile: a wooden pole driven into the bottom of the Venice waterways and used to support buildings and other structures.

plague: a highly contagious and deadly disease.

portrait: a picture of a person, especially one showing only the face or head and shoulders.

posterity: all succeeding generations.

precise: exact or detailed.

procession: a group of people moving along in the same direction, to the same place, or for the same reason.

profusion: an overpowering quantity or amount.

prolific: producing many works.

proportions: the balanced relationships between parts of a whole.

realist: someone who produces realistic art that looks like the thing it represents.

rebel: to fight against authority or a person who fights against authority.

recurring: happening over again.

Renaissance: the period in European history between the 1300s and 1700 that was marked by dramatic social, political, artistic, and scientific change.

repent: to feel regret for an action.

restoration: to bring something back into a former position or condition.

rival: a competitor.

Roman Empire: the large empire centered in Rome, in present-day Italy, that was founded in 753 BCE, according to legend.

scaffolding: a system of platforms used to reach high places.

sculpture: the art of making two- or three-dimensional representations of forms, especially by carving wood or stone or by casting metal or plaster.

secular: not religious.

sfumato: a way of adding shading to a painting.

stroke: a lack of oxygen to part of the brain caused by the blocking or breaking of a blood vessel.

subtle: delicate and elusive.

symbolic: something that stands for or represents something else.

tempera: a paint made from mixing together egg yolks, water, and finely ground pigments for color.

temple: a building used as a place of religion.

texts: pieces of writing.

titan: an important person.

tondo: a circular painting.

typify: to represent by an image, form, or model.

vegetarian: someone who doesn't eat meat.

versatile: able to be used in a lot of ways.

virtue: any good quality or trait.

BOOKS

- Carr, Simonetta. *Michelangelo for Kids: His Life and Ideas, with 21 Activities.* Chicago Review Press, 2016.

- Greenblatt, Stephen. *The Swerve: How the World Became Modern.* W.W. Norton & Co., 2011.

- Langley, Andrew. *DK Eyewitness Books: Da Vinci And His Times.* DK Children, 2006.

- Nichols, Tom. *Renaissance Art: A Beginner's Guide.* Oneworld Publications, 2015.

- Phillips, John. *Leonardo da Vinci: The Genius Who Defined the Renaissance.* National Geographic World History Biographies, 2006.

VIDEO

- *Art of the Northern Renaissance.* Teaching Company, 2005.

- Khan Academy

- *Leonardo da Vinci: The Universal Genius.* Kultur, 2011.

- *Medici: Godfathers of the Renaissance.* Lion Television, 2003.

- *Sister Wendy's The Story of Painting.* BBC, 1999.

- *The Titan: Story of Michelangelo.* Directed by Robert Snyder, 2015.

MUSEUMS BY COUNTRY

United States

- Art Institute of Chicago
  artic.edu

- Cleveland Museum of Art
  clevelandart.org

- Detroit Institute of Art
  dia.org

- Georgia Museum of Art
  georgiamuseum.org

- Isabella Stewart Gardner Museum
  gardnermuseum.org

- Kimbell Art Museum
  kimbellart.org

- Metropolitan Museum of Art
  metmuseum.org

- Museum of Fine Arts
  mfa.org

- National Gallery of Art, Washington, DC
  nga.org

- Norton Simon Museum
  nortonsimon.org

Italy

- Uffizzi Gallery Museum
  uffizi.org

- Accademia Gallery
  accademia.org

- Bargello Museum
  uffizi.com/bargello-national-museum-florence.asp

- The Sistine Chapel
  museivaticani.va/content/museivaticani/en/collezioni/musei/cappella-sistina.html

- The Gallery of the Academy of Florence
  accademia.org

MUSEUMS BY COUNTRY (CONTINUED)

France

· Louvre Museum: louvre.fr/en

England

· National Gallery, London nationalgallery.org.uk

Spain

· Museo del Prado: museodelprado.es/en

Russia

· Hermitage Museum hermitagemuseum.org/wps/ portal/hermitage/?lng=en

Switzerland

· Kunst Museum Basel: kunstmuseumbasel.ch

Austria

· Kunsthistorisches Museum: khm.at

Germany

· Gameldegalerie Alte Meister gemaeldegalerie.skd.museum/ en

QR CODE GLOSSARY

PAGE 8: history.com/topics/ancient-history/ ancient-greece/videos/ancient-greek-art

PAGE 14: youtube.com/watch?v=WIueunmWQjs

PAGE 19: youtube.com/watch?v=XYTT3U9Fhiw

PAGE 20: youtube.com/watch?v=9ODhKqFaugQ

PAGE 25: oddee.com/item_99742.aspx

PAGE 36: khanacademy.org/humanities/ap-art-history/ early-europe-and-colonial-americas/ renaissance-art-europe-ap/v/ leonardo-da-vinci-last-supper-1495-98

PAGE 43: youtube.com/watch?v=RpZ1TwGaugM

PAGE 50: museumsinflorence.com/musei/ medici_riccardi_palace.html

PAGE 54: khanacademy.org/humanities/ renaissance-reformation/high-ren-florence-rome/ michelangelo/v/michelangelo-piet-1498-1500

PAGE 56: youtube.com/watch?v=M_uvmQ-XdJo

PAGE 58: khanacademy.org/humanities/ ap-art-history/early-europe-and-colonial-americas/ renaissance-art-europe-ap/v/ michelangelo-ceiling-of-the-sistine-chapel-1508-12

PAGE 63: youtube.com/watch?v=46_wiOboDk4

PAGE 70: khanacademy.org/humanities/ renaissance-reformation/high-ren-florence-rome/ high-renaissance1/v/raphael-marriage-of-the-virgin-1504

PAGE 73: youtube.com/watch?v=d1i4VvEma5Y

PAGE 77: youtube.com/watch?v=Smd-q44ysoM

PAGE 87: dailymotion.com/video/x2ofhyh

PAGE 90: khanacademy.org/humanities/ renaissance-reformation/renaissance-venice/ late-renaissance-venice/v/titian-assumption-of-the-virgin

PAGE 97: youtube.com/watch?v=FBf7OFUoKsc

A

activities (Project)
Analyze a Work of Art, 23
Collaborative Creations, 63
Compare and Contrast, 24,
44–45, 62, 80, 96
The Human Body in Art, 43
Patronage and Public Art, 97
Responding to *The Birth of Venus*,
25
The School of Athens, 81
Adoration of the Magi (da Vinci),
28, 31
The Adoration of the Magi
(Botticelli), 10, 12, 14–15, 23
An Allegory of Prudence (Titian), 94
Anguissola, Sofonisba, 60
apprenticeships, 4
Arnolfini Portrait (van Eyck), 2, 20
Assumption of the Virgin (Titian), 3,
84, 88–90
Athanasius, 92

B

Bacchus (Michelangelo), 48, 53, 62
Bacchus and Ariadne (Titian), 85,
92–93
The Baptism of Christ (Verrocchio),
44
Bartolomeo Colleoni statue
(Verrocchio), 30
The Battle of Anghiari (da Vinci),
29, 71
Battle of Cascina (Michelangelo),
49, 71
Bellini, Gentile, 84, 86
Bellini, Giovanni, 84, 86, 89, 90
Benois Madonna (da Vinci), 80
Bihzad, Kamal al-din, 61
The Birth of Venus (Botticelli), 13,
18–19, 25

Bosch, Hieronymus, 2, 41
Botticelli, Sandro, 10–25
early years and family of, 12, 14,
16
legacy of, 22
mythological subjects of, 11–12,
16–20, 25
regrets of, possible, 20–21
religious subjects of, 11–16, 21,
22, 23–24
timelinc of, 12–13
Titian comparison to, 96
The Adoration of the Magi, 10, 12,
14–15, 23
The Birth of Venus, 13, 18–19, 25
The Mystical Nativity, 13, 24
Portrait of a Young Woman, 11
Primavera, 2, 13, 17
Sistine Chapel frescoes, 13, 22
The Temptations of Christ, 22
Bruegel, Pieter, the Elder, 3

C

Caprotti de Oreno, Gian Giacomo
"Salai," 37
Cavalieri, Tommaso de, 59
cherubs (Raphael), 2, 78
The Chess Game (Anguissola), 60
Church Militant (Athanasius), 92
Coatlicue statue, 68
commissions and contracts, 9
Conte, Jacopino del, 46
The Creation of Adam
(Michelangelo), 47, 58
cupid, fake (Michelangelo), 48, 52
Cupid with Wheel of Fortune
(Titian), 1

D

David (Michelangelo), 3, 49,
54–56, 61, 71

da Vinci, Leonardo, 26–45
companion and assistant of, 40
drawings and sketches of, 28, 43
early years and family of, 28, 29,
37
experimental techniques of, 34,
36
human body in art of, 7, 28, 43,
60
legacy of, 41–42
in Milan, 28, 31–32, 33, 34–37
military engineering and
inventions of, 32, 37
portrait/self-portrait of, 26, 27,
40
Raphael influenced by, 67, 71–74,
80
religious subjects of, 28–29, 31,
32–37, 42, 44–45, 71, 80
teacher of, 28, 29–30
timeline of, 28–29
unfinished works of, 27, 28,
31–32, 37, 39, 42, 71
Adoration of the Magi, 28, 31
The Battle of Anghiari, 29, 71
Benois Madonna, 80
Gran Cavallo (Great Horse), 32
The Last Supper, 2, 29, 34–37, 71
Mona Lisa, vi, 1, 29, 37–39, 73
St. John the Baptist, 44
Salvator Mundi, 42
The Virgin of the Rocks, 29, 32–34
The Vitruvian Man, 7
The Deposition (Raphael), 74–75
Dogon art, 21
Dome of Santa Maria del Popolo
(Raphael), 65
Doni, Agnolo and Maddalena, 66,
72–74
Doni Tondo (Michelangelo), 74
La Donna Velata (Raphael), 73
Duccio, 6
Dürer, Albrecht, 2, 59

E

Elizabeth I of England (Teerlinc), 16

Equestrian Portrait of Charles V (Titian), 85, 88

F

The Fall of Phaeton (Michelangelo), 59

Feast of Herod (Lippi), 13

Fontana, Lavinia, 42

Francis I (king), 37, 42

frescoes, 4, 13, 16, 22, 29, 50, 51, 57, 67, 71, 84

G

Galizia, Fede, 5, 77

The Garden of Earthly Delights (Bosch), 2, 41

Gentileschi, Artemisia, 95

Ghirlandaio, Domenico, 50

Giorgione, 84, 86–87, 91

The Girlhood of Mary Virgin (Rossetti), 79

Gran Cavallo (Great Horse) (da Vinci), 32

Greek influences, 2–3, 4, 6, 17, 19, 55

H

Hercules at the Crossroad (Dürer), 59

human body, in art, 6–7, 28, 43, 49, 55, 60, 61, 74. *See also* nudity, in art

humanism, 4–5

J

Judith Slaying Holofernes (Gentileschi), 95

Julius II (pope), 49, 56–57, 66, 67, 71, 75, 78

K

Kano Masanobu/Kano School of Painting, 39

L

The Last Judgment (Michelangelo), 49

The Last Supper (da Vinci), 2, 29, 34–37, 71

Leo X (pope), 37, 41, 67

Lippi, Filippo, 12–13

M

Madonna and Child (Santi), 67

Madonna of the Pinks (Raphael), 67, 80

Maiolica Basket of Fruit (Galizia), 5

Male Nude, Turning to the Right (Michelangelo), 49

A Man with a Quilted Sleeve (Titian), 88

Marriage of Mary (Ghirlandaio), 50

Marriage of the Virgin (Perugino), 69–70

The Marriage of the Virgin (Raphael), 66, 69–70

Medici family, 13, 14, 16–19, 22, 48, 50–51

medieval art, 5–6

Melone, Altobello, 8

Melzi, Francesco, 40

Michelangelo, 46–63
   Cavalieri as love of, 59
   early years and family of, 48–50, 56
   human body in art of, 49, 55, 60, 61, 74
   legacy of, 61
   Medici relationship with, 48, 50–51
   personality and personal characteristics of, 47–48, 52–53, 56, 59–60
   portrait of, 46
   Raphael influenced by, 71, 74
   religious subjects of, 47, 48–49, 54–55, 57–58, 61, 74
   reputation of, 53–56
   timeline of, 48–49
   Bacchus, 48, 53, 62

Battle of Cascina, 49, 71

The Creation of Adam, 47, 58

David, 3, 49, 54–56, 61, 71

Doni Tondo, 74

fake cupid, 48, 52

The Fall of Phaeton, 59

Julius II tomb sculptures, 49, 56–57, 71

The Last Judgment, 49

Male Nude, Turning to the Right, 49

Pietà, 48, 53–54, 61

Sistine Chapel ceiling, 3, 47, 49, 57–58, 61

Minerva Dressing (Fontana), 42

Mona Lisa (da Vinci), vi, 1, 29, 37–39, 73

The Mystical Nativity (Botticelli), 13, 24

mythology, in art, 8, 9, 11–12, 16–20, 25, 59, 85, 92–93

N

nudity, in art, 6, 19, 42, 49, 55

P

paints, types of, 14, 20, 34, 36

patrons of artists, 9, 97. *See also specific patrons*

Perugino, Pietro, 68–70

Pesaro Madonna (Titian), 85, 90–91

Pietà (Michelangelo), 48, 53–54, 61

Poesie (Titian), 85

Portrait of a Gentleman (Melone), 8

Portrait of a Young Woman (Botticelli), 11

Portrait of Doge Leonardo Loredan (Bellini), 86

Portrait of Leonardo (Melzi), 40

Portrait of Michelangelo (Conte), 46

portraits, 8, 16, 32, 60, 66, 67, 72–74, 77, 86. *See also* self-portraits; *specific portraits*

Primavera (Botticelli), 2, 13, 17

R

Raphael, 64–81
da Vinci's influence on, 67, 71–74, 80
early years and family of, 66, 67–68
in Florence, 66, 70, 71–74
human body in art of, 74
legacy of, 79
Michelangelo's influence on, 71, 74
religious subjects of, 6, 65, 66–67, 69–70, 74–76, 78, 80
reputation and success of, 65–66, 69–79
romantic ties of, 73
self-portrait of, 64, 78
teachers of, 68–70
timeline of, 66–67
in the Vatican, 75–77
cherubs, 2, 78
The Deposition, 74–75
Dome of Santa Maria del Popolo, 65
Doni portraits, 66, 72–74
La Donna Velata, 73
Madonna of the Pinks, 67, 80
The Marriage of the Virgin, 66, 69–70
The School of Athens, 3, 67, 76–78, 81
The Sistine Madonna, 78
Virgin Mary and Child, 6
religion
medieval approach to, 5–6, 9
Renaissance approach to, 2, 4, 6, 9. *See also under specific artists*
Renaissance
artists of. *See* Renaissance artists
defining the, 1, 2, 4
human body in art of, 6–7. *See also* human body, in art
humanism during, 4–5
medieval art before, 5–6
subject of art during, 8
timeline of, 2–3. *See also under specific artists*

Renaissance artists
Botticelli as, 2, 10–25, 96
as celebrities, 9
commissions and contracts with, 9
da Vinci as, vi, 1, 2, 7, 26–45, 60, 67, 71–74, 80
Michelangelo as, 3, 46–63, 71, 74
patrons of, 9, 97
Raphael as, 2, 3, 6, 64–81
Titian as, 1, 3, 82–97
women as, 9, 16, 42, 60, 77, 95
Roman influences, 2, 4, 6, 17, 55
Rossetti, Dante, 79

S

St. John the Baptist (da Vinci), 44
St. John the Evangelist (Titian), 83
Salvator Mundi (da Vinci), 42
Santi, Giovanni, 66, 67, 68
Savonarola, Girolamo, 13, 20–21
The School of Athens (Raphael), 3, 67, 76–78, 81
The Seduction of Yusuf (Bihzad), 61
Self-Portrait as the Allegory of Painting (Gentileschi), 95
self-portraits, 8, 9, 10, 26, 27, 60, 64, 78, 82, 95
Sforza, Ludovico, 32, 34–35
Sistine Chapel
ceiling (Michelangelo), 3, 47, 49, 57–58, 61
frescoes (Botticelli), 13, 22
The Last Judgment (Michelangelo), 49
The Sistine Madonna (Raphael), 78
Still Life (Galizia), 77

T

Teerlinc, Levina, 16
The Tempest (Giorgione), 87
The Temptations of Christ (Botticelli), 22
Titian, 82–97
color, composition, and techniques of, 84, 88–91, 93, 95–96

early years and family of, 84, 85, 90, 94
Giorgione collaboration with, 84, 86–87, 91
legacy of, 95
mythological subjects of, 85, 92–93
portraits/self-portraits by, 82, 85, 88
religious subjects of, 83, 84–85, 88–91
teachers and apprenticeships of, 84, 86
timeline of, 84–85
in Venice, 83–85, 88–91, 94–95
An Allegory of Prudence, 94
Assumption of the Virgin, 3, 84, 88–90
Bacchus and Ariadne, 85, 92–93
Cupid with Wheel of Fortune, 1
Equestrian Portrait of Charles V, 85, 88
A Man with a Quilted Sleeve, 88
Pesaro Madonna, 85, 90–91
Poesie, 85
St. John the Evangelist, 83
Venus of Urbino, 3, 85

V

van Eyck, Jan, 2, 20
Vecellio, Orazio, 94
Venus of Urbino (Titian), 3, 85
Verrocchio, 28, 29–30, 44
Virgin in Glory with Saints (Bellini), 89, 90
Virgin Mary and Child (Duccio), 6
Virgin Mary and Child (Raphael), 6
Virgin of the Rocks (da Vinci), 29, 32–34
The Vitruvian Man (da Vinci), 7

W

women, as Renaissance artists, 9, 16, 42, 60, 77, 95

Z

Zuccato, Sebastian, 84, 86